Towards a Theory of Drama in Education

Gavin M. Bolton MA, LRAM, ADB
University of Durham, England

Longman

LONGMAN GROUP LIMITED
London
*Associated companies, branches and representatives
throughout the world*

First published 1979
ISBN 0 582 36137 0 cased
0 582 36138 9 paper

Printed in Hong Kong
by Wing Tai Cheung Printing Co Ltd

Contents

Acknowledgements

I have been lucky throughout my career in meeting and being guided by so many remarkable people. First and foremost I am indebted to Dorothy Heathcote who has been and I hope will continue to be for a long time my friend and mentor. I shall never catch up with her genius, but I enjoy the chase!

My special thanks are due to David Davis and Geoff Gillham on whose support and sound judgement I have depended so often. I cannot name all who have helped me, but I must acknowledge John Allen, David Clegg, Chris Day, Walter Ellis, John Fines, John Garner, Merica Goodall, John Merritt, Mary Robson, Ann Shaw, Veronica Sherbourne, Ray Verrier, Pat Yates and my colleagues in the University of Durham. And I shall always be indebted to Peter Slade and Brian Way without whose inspiration I would not have turned to drama in education.

Finally my thanks go to Cecily, Deirdre, Kathy, Albert, Derek and Tony, Durham's MA (Ed.) Drama students who, in taking their degree course between October and June 1977/78, spent a great deal of their time challenging and encouraging me through the writing of these chapters.

Gavin Bolton

This book is dedicated to Norah Morgan, the brilliant Ontario teacher who through many beautiful summers hammered out this book with me long before we realised it was one.

Introduction

This is not an academic book. It is backed only by personal experience, not by research. Nor is it concerned with giving tips for teachers. Anyone hoping to learn how to teach drama from it will be frustrated. Indirectly, however, I hope it will still help the inexperienced teacher, for it is a discussion of principles. It is with the student-teacher in mind that at the end of some of the chapters I have posed a number of questions.

In the main, however, I see the book as a continuation of a dialogue with experienced teachers, especially those teachers who have watched me teach and helped me to learn what I know – and what I don't know.

As an attempt to devise a theory of drama in education this publication is but a beginning – hence the appropriate tentativeness of the title. My guess is that whereas some aspects of my thinking will be productive, others will lead into a cul-de-sac. I am too close to the work at the moment to distinguish between the two. I look forward to the dialogue continuing.

G.B.

1 Classification of dramatic activity

It is not easy to write about children's drama. As I put words on paper I see all kinds of actions of past drama lessons in my head. For the reader there is the danger that the words remain just as words or, worse still, become subtly stretched to apply to quite a different set of actions in the reader's head. I have attended so many conferences where, in the early stages, members have vigorously nodded to each other in mutual agreement only to discover much later that they have been speaking from totally different conceptual frameworks in spite of using the same vocabulary. I hope gradually to make clear the kind of educational drama activities that interest me. If these are completely outside your experience you may feel like a traditional mathematician reading a book on new maths or a formal sixth-form teacher attempting to study the principles underlying informal education in the primary school. I hope, however, that the uninitiated will be helped by the many illustrative examples throughout the book and that those who are already familiar with this approach to drama teaching will appreciate and benefit from the main purpose of this book, which is an attempt to clarify a philosophy of drama in education in order to sharpen its practice.

Although many able people have written about educational drama, I do not propose to use their publications as my points of reference. It seems to me this would trap me into a discussion of what other people *think* about drama, whereas I want to confine myself here to what theories may be drawn from a certain kind of contemporary practice. If I refer to other people at all it will, in the main, be from an appreciation of what they *do* in drama. Most of the examples of practice will be from my own teaching – the good *and* the bad. Sometimes it is easier to make a theoretical point from one's

1

mistakes, especially where those mistakes go beyond mere errors of judgement to wrong or misunderstood principles. I have made, and still make, many mistakes when working with children, but I happen to be blessed with those two contradictory qualities essential perhaps for all drama teachers – a humility to recognise my mistakes combined with an arrogance of certainty that I can not only learn from them but also abstract a sufficiently firm philosophy from the experience to write a book about it!

One of my strengths may be that I have taught drama in a variety of different ways. Teachers of my generation have been subjected to many different professional whims and fashions and I have been variously a drama teacher with a script, a tambour, a story, a record, or a list of mime exercises or jingles in my hand or, in the heady days of free expression, nothing at all in my hand – nor in my head either! Only more recently has my drama teaching become symbolised by a piece of chalk in the hand, but more of that later.

In this chapter I attempt a classification of the main kinds of drama experiences that are promoted in schools and colleges – not a conventional classification into speech, movement, improvisation, and so on. My purpose is to provide a reference point, so that if the reader has had any drama experience at all some of the activities in the list will be easily recognisable and when I later attempt to relate these activities to my present philosophy, a 'way in' to the different perspective will have been provided. The basic experience of drama offered to children and college students falls into three major orientations:

Type A: Exercise;
Type B: Dramatic playing;
Type C: Theatre.

It would be misleading for me to claim that these are watertight categories. It is possible to think of many instances which do not fall easily under a particular heading. Indeed I shall later be making the point that the kind of drama I am advocating (would it be useful to label it Type D drama?) can be served, albeit with a significantly different emphasis, by all three kinds of experience. I shall now analyse these categories further, breaking them into sub-categories where necessary.

Type A: Exercise

It is possible to distinguish five kinds of exercise in common usage in drama teaching. Some teachers tend to keep to a particular kind, for instance, games or technical skills. My purpose is to identify the chief characteristics of 'exercise' as a concept in drama. Below therefore is a catalogue of examples from which we can isolate distinguishing features.

I. Directly experiential
  i Going into a dark cellar, i.e. in *actuality*.
 ii Interviewing people in the street, i.e. in *actuality*.
iii Watching workers in the fish market.
 iv Listening to sounds outside in the street.
  v In pairs; one partner trying to stop the other getting off the floor by sitting on him.
 vi Any 'relaxing', 'limbering up' or 'concentration' exercise.
vii Skipping to a drum-beat.

II. Dramatic skill practice
  i Recalling smell of musty cellar.
 ii Working at a 'Richard III' walk.
iii Imagining sounds outside in the street.
 iv Brandishing a sword (real or imaginary) so that it says 'Victory', 'Defeat', 'Revenge', 'Slaughter of the Innocents', 'Peace'.
  v Practising the intonation for role of a priest.
 vi Selecting the appropriate vocabulary and style of phrasing in preparation for the 'royal declaration'.

III. 'Drama' exercise
  i To teacher's narration: 'And suddenly you find yourself in a dark cellar ... you can smell the damp and feel the cold ... when I tap the tambour you see something shin-

    ing in the corner . . . you hesitate . . . you move nearer'
    etc.

ii   A and B in pairs holding an interview practice, with one
    as interviewer and the other as interviewee.

iii The situation is: Daughter wants to leave home. Father
    disapproves; mother approves. Find out how your group
    deals with the problem.

iv I want you to act out the story I've just read (*The Pied
    Piper of Hamelin*) and see if you can remember every-
    thing that happens.

IV. Games
  i   The active: 'Stick-in-the-mud'.
  ii The concentrating: 'Buzz'.
 iii The skilful: 'Chinese sticks'.
 iv The competitive: most ball games.
  v The group-cohesive: 'St Peter's keys'.

V. Other art forms
  i   Tell the story so far.
  ii Write the story so far.
 iii Design the family crest.
 iv Draw what you think will happen when you enter the
    haunted house.
  v Composing the 'Peace' song.
 vi Creating the harvest dance.
 vii Taking a photograph of the slum street.
viii Filming passers-by.

The above list of exercises, long as it is, does not cover all
the possible types but there are enough examples for me
now to discuss why all the above activities can be labelled as
'exercises'. Indeed many teachers whose lessons are made up
entirely of such experiences would argue that they are doing
drama with their classes, the implication behind their defence
being that 'exercise' is an inferior category of experience. All
three forms of dramatic activity: exercise, dramatic playing
and theatre, have, in educational terms, their limitations and
their strengths. This book is concerned with exploring in

what ways a teacher may use any of these forms so that the strengths are harnessed and the limitations reduced. It suffices at this stage to say that any exclusive use of a particular form invites a deteriorating educational experience progressively relying on the weaknesses within the form.

An extreme example of this occurred a few years ago when I discovered during the examination of a final secondary school practice not only that the drama students had prepared for my visit lessons made up entirely of games, but that games had been offered as the only material for drama lessons throughout the length of the school practice.

Let us examine what characteristics might distinguish the above activities as exercises. The reader should avoid putting a 'value' on these characteristics. They take on a value when the educational context is known. For instance, the fact that 'direction cannot be changed' (see no. 6 below) may make an exercise useful in controlling a group of scatter-brains but quite inappropriate for a group of rigid conformists. It will be noticed that a few features apply to all the types of exercises; others relate to certain types; yet others apply only some of the time; some are tendencies rather than static positions.

1 Always short-term; often there is a sense of completion.
2 Always a specific goal often known to both teacher and participants.
3 Sometimes an answer to be found.
4 Always has a 'cutting-off' point, when there is nothing to be gained by continuing, as the participants have reached the required goal. (It is interesting to note, in passing, how many teachers are reluctant to stop an activity although a goal is reached.)
5 Always some kind of instructions, most often preceding the activity, occasionally simultaneous (*see* IIIi), most often given by teacher.
6 It is always understood that the direction cannot be changed (just as in doing a spelling exercise it is not expected that the participant will switch to punctuation).
7 The 'rules' are usually clear.
8 Often it is easily repeatable. (Note this does not apply to

5

the more complex examples in I. Directly experiential.)

9 Usually there is clarity of outward form: an observer would normally be able to recognise fairly quickly what the exercise was about.

10 Usually the exercise is conducted in small groups, pairs or individually.

11 Sometimes the participants' mode of action has a 'demonstrating' quality: the action is *referring* to an idea or a resolution as opposed to 'experiencing'. (This is a very popular form of dramatic action in our secondary schools where in small groups the adolescents think up some social problem and translate it into dramatic form, *demonstrating* their thinking.)

12 Not normally associated with a high degree of emotion. (Note the possible exceptions here are Ii. and Iii.) There are unlikely to be surprises.

13 Most often requires the participants to apply a high level of concentration and energy until the goal is reached.

14 Sometimes problem-solving in form.

To the question, 'What is an exercise in drama?' there is obviously no simple answer. There is an amalgam of structural, educational and psychological features that distinguishes it from Types B and C.

Let us now look at the second basic form:

Type B: Dramatic playing

Although later (in chapter 4) I make a distinction between children's make-believe play and 'dramatic playing', they are characteristically so close to each other that for the purposes of this chapter we can regard them as the same activity except that dramatic playing takes place in a school, has the blessing of the school and is often called drama by both children and teacher.

i Fixed by place: Wendy house, hospital, fortress, supermarket, space-ship.

ii Fixed by situation: family life, school life, army life, camping.

6

III Fixed by anticipation of gang-fighting: cowboys and Indians, Northern Ireland, Germans and Allies.

IV Fixed by anticipation of elemental disaster: shipwreck, climbing Everest.

V Fixed by story-line: *The Pied Piper of Hamelin*.

VI Fixed by character-study. An extreme example of this occurred in an adult short-course where the students were asked to arrive 'in character' and to sustain those roles throughout the weekend.

I am sure teachers will recognise many aspects of this basic Type B drama. Let us look closely at its principal features.

1 Not limited to time; indeed 'when to finish' is rarely clear.

2 No specific goal; often no sense of completion.

3 Any limitations are imposed by consensus and are changeable.

4 The principal qualities are fluidity, flexibility and spontaneity.

5 The rules are not always clear.

6 The experience is not easily repeatable.

7 Lacks a clarity of outward form – an observer might find it difficult to recognise what it was about.

8 Usually conducted in small groups.

9 Often the mode of action is an intense 'living-through' (as opposed to *demonstrating* ideas) very occasionally close to life-pace. An existential quality.

10 Level of thinking often shallow, governed by 'what-should-happen-next?' mentality.

11 It does not *require* a high level of emotion and concentration but they sometimes occur.

12 Energy level is usually high.

13 Can 'survive' changeable degrees of individual co-operation and commitment.

14 Freedom for individual creativity; sometimes that creativity is stifled by the low common denominator of group consensus.

15 Three elements are necessary to the experience: a sequence of actions (plot); defined place or persons

7

(context); and a source of energy, motivation or centre of interest (hidden theme).

Whereas the list of features distinguishing Type A, Exercise, was an attempt to find the common factors in an extremely disparate collection of activities, Type B's examples represent a distinct activity for which it is comparatively easy to formulate a list of characteristics. The last item on the Type B list, the 'three elements necessary to the experience', is discussed further (in chapter 3) as the central characteristic of Type D drama. In this kind of drama there are always two levels of content: explicitly, the content provided by plot and context and, implicitly, the content provided by personal wants, beliefs, attitudes of the participants. This I have called the 'hidden theme'. For example:

Plot-context	Hidden theme
1 Cowboys and Indians	Determination to win
2 High-jacking plane	Wanting to show off 'acting' skills

It will be noticed that the 'hidden theme' in the first example is more compatible with plot and context than in the second. This fascinating area of compatibility of meanings is pursued later (in chapter 4) but opening up the topic here allows me to draw attention to a significant, perhaps the most significant, difference in emphasis between Type A and Type B drama. On the whole (there are important exceptions) a teacher working in Type A will tend to emphasise form whereas a teacher working in Type B will be more aware of content. It is the teacher who is aware of not the explicit but the implicit, hidden themes in his pupils' work who has the greatest chance of understanding the principles of Type D drama.

Type C: Theatre

First let us examine the concept of Type C. Illustrations can fall nicely along an informal/formal continuum. Each example is concerned with sharing with an audience, for that is what theatre is. It can be argued that the first example fails to meet that particular requirement.

I The head-teacher or the class next door 'drop in' to see the children's drama work.

II Showing each other plays improvised by small groups or (as in Exercise IIIiii), the resolution of a problem.

III Working at polishing a story, say *The Pied Piper of Hamelin*, ready for an end-of-term showing to small or large, informal or formal audience.

IV Working at a play script for the purpose of showing to an audience.

The principal features are:

1 Demand for clarity in speech and action.
2 The external features of the action must convey the meaning of the play or story.
3 Skill lies in pretending (naturalistic) or demonstrating (Brechtian) a reality.
4 Demands high degree of commitment and co-operation.
5 Strengths and weaknesses, *especially* weaknesses, become highlighted.
6 There is often a strong sense of an 'event', which positively affects both players and non-players in a school.
7 All work geared to the importance of the 'end-product'. Can bring exhilarating sense of achievement.

No survey has been done as far as I know on which of the three types of drama is the most popular. There is probably a sizeable proportion of drama teachers in this country who work exclusively towards Type C. The number of nativity plays, large-scale secondary school productions and the content of CSE and GCE syllabuses provide some evidence of this. But in my experience a great deal of theatre-type work is done as drama in schools even when there is no final performance in mind. Children are taught to perform *as if* there were an audience, that is, they are trained to look at themselves from the outside ready for their hypothetical audience. This kind of work is fed by books such as Penny Whittam's *Teaching Speech and Drama in the Infant School* (1977), where, although the author talks about 'free-expression', such a concept is denied by many of the exercises which take on a theatre form as she makes it more and more evident that she thinks in terms of 'externals'.

It will be useful at this stage to underline the main differences between the three types by taking an example that has cropped up in all three. I am referring to the very popular story form which teachers use in quite contrasting ways. I have deliberately instanced the same story in each list, *The Pied Piper of Hamelin*, so that we can make comparison. Now, if the teacher emphasises the importance of remembering the facts in sequence as a way of getting the children to know the story, or if the children practise scurrying round the hall soundlessly as rats, or if in pairs they design new rat-traps then the teacher is using exercise. If, on the other hand, the children use the story-line simply as a reference point for their own form of playing then they are in the more fluid Type B. If the children and teacher are concerned with communicating every action and sound to someone else (real or hypothetical) to give a faithful entertaining enactment of the story, then clearly they are working in theatre. Many teachers may use all three kinds of experiences. It is possible that the teacher who is working towards a production may use exercise and even free dramatic playing as early phases in the work. He might have his class experience the infestation of the Hamelin houses through their dramatic playing, thus claiming that he was working in process before going on to product. Unfortunately in practice, even if the teacher leans over backwards not to think in theatre terms for the early phase of the work, if the children have previously had any kind of taste of theatre they will almost certainly bring the memory of that particular perspective to the new piece of work. The teacher may legitimately want the children to experience the quarrelling of the townsfolk as an experience in itself, but the children may have trapped themselves into *demonstrating* a quarrel. The teacher may intend that they dance with uninhibited pleasure to the Piper's tune, but they are out to catch his eye for approval or they are wondering if the dance steps are 'right'. Or there maybe certain children in his class who persist in working in theatre form, just those few who have had a chance to be in the school production or, heaven help us, those who in attending private speech classes, are regularly subjected to a form of examination that uses 'how it seems from the outside' as its principal criterion.

In this chapter I have suggested that there are three basic types of educational drama experience: Type A: Exercise; Type B: Dramatic playing; Type C: Theatre. Although there is some overlap, each is characterised by its cluster of distinguishing features and the classification will have meaning for most teachers. Indeed you may have already placed yourself alongside or bestride certain examples. There will however be some readers whose approach to drama does not fit in with any of the three categories, nor even with a combination of selected aspects. They may feel that what they offer children and students is of a different order of experience from anything outlined so far. This is the claim I make for my own theory and practice of drama-in-education which, for the sake of convenience, I am labelling Type D: Drama for understanding. Let me say straight away there may well be Types E, F, G and Z or there may be many versions of Type D. I also recognise that the very notion of labelling and classifying creative experience can be irritating, if not positively destructive. I am therefore taking a risk, but as I know of no other way of isolating what I want to talk about I have no choice but to ask you to bear with me and to make your own qualifying adjustments as you read.

Questions

1 Traditional divisions of drama have included such categories as improvisation, script work, speech, movement and mime. Discuss the advantages and drawbacks of such a classification.
2 Do you consider the author makes a justifiable distinction between the three orientations? Can you classify your own student drama work in this way?

2 Let's look at a lesson

Examine closely the following lesson notes. They are not invented: they are from an actual lesson with a class of first year secondary school children whom the teacher had not met before, although he was familiar with the school. The notes are designed to help you work out the thinking of the teacher who wrote them. How do you assess this lesson preparation? How does it compare with your own style of teaching?

Lesson one

1 Space on their own (this may need practising).
2 Take them through exercises with hands (cruel, kind, murderous, nervous, *greedy*). Make sure they do the last one well.
3 'Turn whole of yourself into a miser.'
4 'Unlock your door and peep out. Lock it again.'
5 'Sit down; feel under bed; bring out a box; show me the size of it.'
6 'Open it. Count money.'
7 'All count aloud one to ten in normal voice.'
8 'Now change your whole shape into miser's shape and when you count, see if your voice has changed shape.'
9 'Now, at your own pace, play the scene: Miser opening and locking door; getting out box; counting the money (aloud); locking up box; sitting still. (If you finish before other children do, just wait quietly.)'
10 'Find a partner. One of you is the miser; the other is a visitor; something is going to happen; discuss this in pairs; make sure you both know exactly where the door is and where other important items in the room are.'

This is a classic example of exercise oriented teaching. What can we learn further about this teacher?

1 Space on their own (this may need practising). This teacher is concerned with order and his own security.

2 Exercises with hands.
He works for concentration and for external appearance. Looking at own hands also reduces self-consciousness – the children cannot catch each other's eyes.

2 Make sure they do the last one (greedy) well. I wonder what his criteria for 'doing well' are? Suspect choice of subject matter is more to do with his sense of order (a scene with one person, a miser, in it) rather than for any other educational reason. He may be tied to the false educational concept so fervently preached by people who published books on how to teach drama that there is a natural progression for children in first working on their own before they move to sharing in pairs and then in small groups. The only validity I can recognise and respect in this is if the children involved are by temperament destroyers of each other's work or if the teacher only feels safe with this particular progression.

Notice the teacher's stereotyping of miser i.e. miser = greedy, a cliché which he then imposes on the pupils.

3, 4, 5 and 6. A series of puppeteer instructions obviously demanding thoughtless obedience. Note the significance of 'Show *me* the size of it'.

7 and 8. Tackle use of voice separately.
There is a logic to this preparation, the logic of a teacher who is not interested in giving the children an 'internal' experience of miser.

9 'Now, at your own pace ...'
Like most exercises, it can be repeated. There is no question of the 'misers' feeling that as they have just counted the money once there is no need to count it again. No one is suggesting, least of all the teacher, that the children have *experienced* that particular miser's action. It is an exercise that somehow will be improved by doing it a second time. Does the teacher have a hypothetical audience in mind? Indeed does it seem

reasonable to assume that they are really doing it for *him*, that he is the audience to whom they will direct their activities (remembering to sit quietly when they have finished)? If so it has virtually become theatre while they once more 'play the scene'.

10 'Find a partner ... something is going to happen ...' An invitation to dramatic playing? Could be, depending on how the children respond. They are required to discuss first – he is not risking complete spontaneity. Constraints on the chances of its turning into a free activity are: (*a*) they did not choose the subject-matter; and (*b*) the preparation up to this point will inevitably have put them in an exercise/theatre straitjacket which is difficult to shake off. If in fact the children do break through to a form of dramatic playing it is likely to be of the shallowest kind for the careful step-by-step preparation has concentrated on modifying body and voice to serve the goal of simulation, that is, an imitation of a miser's actions in a miserly context where accuracy in the presentation of such action is the major criterion.

This is not just a classic example of a teacher working in exercise, it is also a classic example of a teacher working externally. There is an INTERNAL ACTION which has been ignored, the action of feeling and thinking or feeling/thinking as I prefer to term it. It is the internal action that is the major concern of a teacher working in Type D drama. If this teacher had wanted to work internally for his step-by-step preparation he would have to have considered such questions as:

1 What is these children's sterotype view of misers?
2 What is there in a 'miser situation' that is worth their while exploring?
3 What is there in their *emotional* knowing that is already relevant and how can it be harnessed so that they have a miser's *experience*?
4 How should the teacher best direct this experience so that the stereotype image is broken and new understanding takes place?

The slow building implied in 3 towards using what they

already know, not in the factual sense of 'what we know about misers' but in the deeper sense of the *feeling* of hoarding, of ownership, of projecting one's identity on to possessions, of not trusting others, of secrets, etc., as a means of creating a new experience is equivalent to, but qualitatively different from, the preparatory steps in the above lessons. But of course, Type D drama steps are of a totally different order, the more precise meaning of which will, I hope, be gradually made clear in subsequent chapters.

One more comment needs to be made about the lesson. Switching for a moment away from the activity of the children to the medium of drama itself, the 'clay' with which the pupils are working, we can find interesting features that are going to be relevant to our later discussions. The created situation 'means' miser; in order to find that meaning, concrete actions and objects are used: small space, hidden box, locked door, counting money, turning key. This teacher has made a significant selection of ingredients for the drama. There is an enormous potential of 'miser meanings' to be tapped in that short list of actions and objects. It is doubtful how conscious he was of his selection. I suspect that his instruction 'Make sure you both know where the door is' was simply dealing with practicalities rather than the overtones to be released by the experience of two people on opposite sides of a locked door. Nevertheless, consciously or not, he has mixed in those ingredients that will allow the pudding to work. Unfortunately his 'exercise mentality' does not, to carry the metaphor further, allow him to put the pudding in the oven to bake. Still less do the children have a chance of getting anywhere near that oven. Sadly both they and their teacher think that the mixture *is* the cake. 'Isn't drama fun!' they will all agree, and some teachers will add that because it's fun it must be good for them.

The reader may by now be feeling that however misguided, weak and inept this teacher may be, his ineptness cannot match this author's heartlessness in tearing to shreds the work of a fellow drama teacher. I now have to make a confession: I am that teacher. The lesson was mine. I taught it just under twenty years ago and I came across the notes in a recent 'spring-cleaning' bout. My immediate reaction was to disown it. 'No, *I* could not have possibly have taught like that!' My second reaction was to search around for excuses: that the children were particularly difficult, that they could only concentrate on their own, that they were so severely subnormal that they had to be told exactly what to do, that they'd had lots of free dramatic playing and so exercises would make a useful change, or that I was having an off day! The truth was that these were very normal first-year secondary children and I genuinely thought this was a good way to teach drama. It has taken me a long time to realise that what I was teaching was not drama at all.

3 Internal and external action

In the last two chapters I have discussed many kinds of dramatic activities that have only indirect bearing on the principles of this book. I must now start to examine some of the features of 'D'-type drama, the most significant of which is the concept of 'internal action'. I may again appear to move away from drama itself in order to outline a child play model, the understanding of which will be crucial for grasping some fundamental principles of drama in education. Like 'dramatic playing', D-type drama also springs from child play, at least more specifically that particular kind of play referred to by Piaget as symbolic as opposed to practice play. Symbolic play (or make-believe play as I prefer to call it) includes some kind of representation; practice play does not. In the latter form a child might jump backwards and forwards across a stream for sheer physical satisfaction; in symbolic play he might be leaping over the heads of crocodiles. Make-believe play, then, is essentially a mental activity where meaning is created by the symbolic use of actions (in this case, jumping) and objects (his own person and a stream).

External action

Let us begin by looking at the external action of make-believe play. Picture a four-year-old boy playing in the garden, distributing on various flat surfaces a number of seaside buckets which he keeps rushing to fill from the water-tap in the garage. 'What are you doing?' asks his mother. 'Cooking,' he replies and disappears for more water. Had she pressed further the mother might have been told that he was a hotel chef, getting ready for a birthday party by making enormous jellies and trifles. Theatre terminology comes in useful here to classify the playing. The child's first answer, 'Cooking,' was the 'title' of the experience. The 'setting' was a hotel kitchen. And it also has a plot, a story-line: a chef is making jellies for a party. The title, plot and setting make up the external action of the make-believe play. If the child later picks up a doll, applies the hosepipe to it and then dresses it, the sequence might be described as Title: putting baby to bed; Plot: mother baths and dresses baby; Setting: the bathroom. All the 'properties' he uses are, of course, part of the setting: the buckets as saucepans, the doll's clothes as baby clothes. In tabular form it looks like this:

Theatre terminology	*Behaviour (A)*	*Behaviour (B)*
Title	Cooking	Putting baby to bed.
Plot	A sequence of fetching, carrying, mixing, heating and cooling	A sequence of soaping, soaking, powdering, putting on nappies and dressing in night-clothes.
Setting	Hotel kitchen and its utensils.	Bathroom and all the bedtime paraphernalia.

The above table describes the external features of the make-believe. The theatre terminology of title, plot and setting inevitably give us the perspective 'from the outside'. But the fascinating thing about make-believe play is that it has two 'outsides'. Whereas a visitor with imagination might comment, 'That chef is busy in his hotel kitchen making jellies', a behaviourist visitor might, not unreasonably, observe that the child was continually going from the garden to the garage tap in order to fill his toy buckets with water. No one could argue with the accuracy of the latter observer; the first visitor's observation, however, might be a matter of interpretation. In other words, it is the *externalisation* of a mental activity that is being described. It is externalisation of a special kind in that its point of reference is concrete (cooking, for example) and its mode of expression is concrete (actual activities in the garden). The external action of make-believe play, therefore, is the juxtaposition of two concrete worlds. One does not replace the other: both are present and interdependent. It is this interdependence that characterises symbolic play and drama, distinguishing symbolic play from other forms of play and drama from other art forms. As we shall see later, it is the way in which the two contexts inter-relate that dictates the quality of the drama experience.

Let us put the two contents in diagrammatic form, using the 'bathing baby' example:

External action

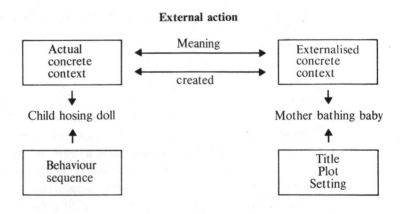

We can use this model of the external action of make-believe play to help us begin to answer the question, 'What is the purpose of play?' It is a model that we can also use in discussing drama in education, the assumption being that the potential in make-believe play for the child is also available, at least in part, to the pupil in drama. A glance at the publications on play will reveal that there are apparently nearly as many reasons for play as there are forms of play. I have, therefore, *selected*: (*a*) that which appears to emerge logically from our external action model; (*b*) that which will provide us with the basis for our future consideration of education objectives in drama; and (*c*) that which has been

19

argued by the eminent Russian psychologist L.S. Vygotsky. Indeed of all writings on play I have found his article, 'Play and its role in the mental development of the child', written in 1933 and translated and published in an excellent collection of writings, *Plays: its role in development and evolution*, edited by Bruner *et al.* (1976), to be perhaps the most useful in terms of relating play to dramatic activity. Not that Vygotsky even mentions such activities: it is his *perspective* on play that I feel can be most usefully applied to the function of drama in education. Unfortunately he, like most play theorists, seems to assume that the need for play atrophies at a certain stage of mental development. What we shall have to argue is that drama activities in school, while using a similar structure, are given a different orientation. Let us in the meantime continue to familiarise ourselves with that structure.

Vygotsky suggests that at a certain stage in the pre-school child's development he progresses from thinking solely in terms of what is present in his perceptual field to thinking beyond what is immediately present. Play is the bridge that allows him to make this change. He cannot 'think' horse if there is no horse present, but by using an object (a stick) and an action of riding the stick, he can begin to 'think' horse. The stick and the action (the actual context) are what he calls 'pivots' to recall the absent object and action (the externalised context). It is interesting to note, in passing, that in his use of the term 'pivot' he is resisting the concept favoured by Piaget that the child uses actions and objects as *symbols* of imagined actions and objects. Vygotsky (1933) writes: 'A child does not symbolise in play, but he wishes and realises his wishes by letting the basic categories of reality pass through his experience, which is precisely why in play a day can take half-an-hour, and a hundred miles are covered in five steps' (p. 550). It may not matter to us at this point whether the stick is a symbol or a pivot. What is important is that the child has this capacity to create MEANING. For Vygotsky, the main function of make-believe play is the predominance of meaning. In saying categorically, 'Action retreats to second place', he is spelling out the paradox that is not only the key to understanding play but the key to putting drama in an educational perspective. 'Drama is doing' we have been told for years by educationists and drama specialists. It seems to me that the power of the medium lies in the more correct notion that 'Drama *seems* to be doing'. It is thought-in-action; its purpose is the creation of meaning; its medium is the interaction between two concrete contexts.

What are the kinds of meanings available from this interaction? They can be classified in many ways. The simplest for our purpose is to divide them into subjective and objective. By subjective I refer to the personal, individual, egocentric, affective meanings that are brought to an experience; by objective I refer to collective, social, impersonal, scientific meanings. Let us pursue the objective aspect.

There are two kinds of meaning springing directly from the external action: sensorimotor skills and objective knowledge. There appear to be two kinds of skills that may be exercised:

1 Skills relevant to the actual context (for instance, the child may carry water in a bucket without spilling it).
2 Skills relevant to the make-believe context (he may practise the vocabulary he thinks the chef uses as he works).

The knowledge available is to do with whatever are the objective facts of the make-believe context. The child brings to light what he already knows about chefs making jellies and trifles and mothers bathing babies; he may adjust or improve that knowledge in the process of playing (he will no doubt quickly learn about garments if he tries putting them on from the wrong end of the doll). This is knowledge literally at first hand. The objective meaning can, as in this case, become refined as a direct result of sensorimotor experience.

But there is a more significant aspect of objective meaning that is available from the playing process that becomes part of the *internal* action. We have seen that in make-believe two concrete contexts are aligned, the one either representing or being a 'pivot' for the other. This juxtaposition becomes impressively clear when the two worlds are far apart, if, for instance, a child uses a stick and says it is a horse. On the other hand there are limits, for, as Vygotsky points out, a child is not likely to use a postcard as a horse. In other words some feature or features of the actual world must be evocative of the created world. But supposing we go to the other extreme, does this tell us anything different? Vygotsky suggests it singles out a fundamental purpose that is not apparent when the two contexts are distinctly separate. If we take an example of the child dressing a doll perhaps we are not so far from mother dressing a baby, and if we take an example of a child actually watering the garden, who says, 'I'm Dad watering the garden', you might think the two contexts are nearly coinciding, but Vygotsky draws on a fascinating example where the two contexts *do* coincide and yet one factor keeps it as make-believe.

Vygotsky describes the experimental work of a colleague (Sully) who one day heard a seven-year-old girl say to her younger sister, 'Let's play sisters'. That this is possible is further evidence of an orientation in play away from action. The girls *are* sisters and they are using the medium of play to detach themselves sufficiently to 'look at being sisters'. They are concerned to explore the 'rules' of the sister relationship that are never made explicit in the business of 'being sisters'. They are being 'made aware' (a phrase popularly and vaguely used by drama teachers which might well carry this more precise meaning). So play is not only *being*. It uses the form of being in order to *explore being*. Essentially, therefore, play is directed towards *abstraction*. Vygotsky concludes: 'From the point of view of development, the fact of creating an imaginary situation can be regarded as a means of developing abstract thought' (p.553).

The abstract level of thought for the sisters was identifying 'sameness'. For the child bathing the doll, it might be 'wetness'; 'filling things' might be the abstraction for the child cooking.

It is true to say then that even when the two contexts appear to coincide, they do not actually do so because of a difference in orientation. There is also a significant difference in structure. If the two girls are to use play to examine themselves as sisters they will have to discipline themselves to a rigorous selection of material for their play: it is only relevant (in this case) to evoke those kinds of actions that emphasise the 'sisterness' of their relationship; the way they dress, the way they stay together, share together. Other episodes not underlying this relationship would have to be discarded. A conscious structuring of the material must take place to meet the demands of moving towards a higher level of abstraction.

A further diagram can usefully summarise at this stage what I have outlined as the external action of make-believe.

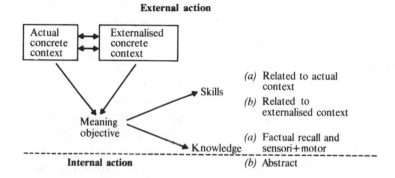

Internal action

In this chapter I have so far discussed what I have termed 'external action', the aspect that is observable at a concrete level. The external action is created from the interaction of two contexts, the actual and the externalised (the make-believe) The participant exercises skills and uses or explores objective knowledge. One aspect of that knowledge, in so far as it is abstracted from the concrete action, can be said to become part of the 'internal' action which we shall discuss now. Internal action is but the other side of the coin, for we are really talking about two aspects of the same experience – it is only for convenience that it has been separated into two identifiable actions.

I hope it will not confuse the reader if I turn to Piaget's terminology here. In *Play, Dreams and Imitations* (1972), Piaget applies the terms primary and secondary symbolism to the two aspects of action, the primary symbolism applying to the child's conscious choice of symbol. Secondary symbolism he describes in the following way:

> But in many games we find symbols whose significance is not understood by the child himself. For instance, a child who has been made jealous by the birth of a younger brother and happens to be playing with two dolls of unequal size, will make the smaller one go away on a journey, while the bigger one stays with its mother. Assuming that the child is unaware that he is thinking of his younger brother and himself, we shall call a case of this kind secondary or unconscious symbolism (p. 171).

If we once again apply theatre terminology we could call 'jealousy of new brother' the theme or the sub-text of the outward action. Just as in dramatic terms title, plot and setting are incomplete without theme, which supplies the underlying meaning of the play, so the activity of the child has an *internal* aspect which controls the meaning of the behaviour. It represents the individual's attitude to his world based on his feelings about the world. As Piaget points out, those feelings are often contradictory. For the sake of clarity they are discussed here as if it is possible to isolate them; indeed it may be reasonable to assume that often a particular feeling predominates.

Let us examine the example of the jealous child. He is unconsciously concerned with his relationship with the new baby. His feeling/judgement of the situation is that 'the new baby is a threat'. The only way the child has of articulating that attitude is through action, in this case the action of make-believe play. The orientation in internal action, therefore, is from the general to the particular, from the theme to the plot as it were. This is the opposite orientation to the external action which moves from the particular to the general. Just as in Vygotsky's example of the two sisters abstracting 'sameness', in Piaget's illustration the child appears to be abstracting (predominantly) size difference and going away, in that it is the smaller of the two dolls he makes go on a journey. There is a recognisable congruence therefore between the objective and subjective features of his play. Diagrammatically it looks like this:

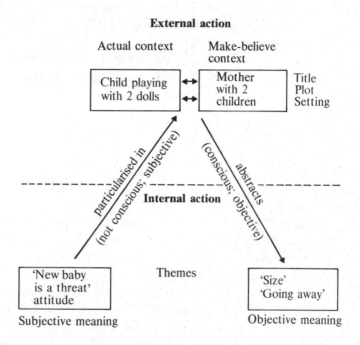

I appreciate this is beginning to look confusedly complex, yet I believe that once grasped it will help the reader to identify the drama principles to which it is related. (If any reader is beginning to doubt its relevance to drama, translate this example of child play into a playwright tackling the theme of the Prodigal Son – from the point of view of the brother!)

In order to make the same points differently let us imagine there were four observers of this doll play: a questioner, an intelligent observer, the child's mother and an unintelligent observer. A dialogue takes place between the questioner and the child.

25

The child chooses two dolls from his collection.

Questions	What are you playing?
Child	I'm their mother. (TITLE)
Questions	What are their names?
Child	Don't know.
Questions	What are you doing with that one?
Child	I'm putting his coat on. (He just makes a vague gesture with the smaller doll's arms. (PLOT)
Questions	Why?
Child	He's going on a train. (He swiftly moves the doll to the other end of the table. (PLOT)
Child	He's gone. (PLOT)

Intelligent observer's comments: 1. 'Although he spoke of "putting coat on" and of "train" the accompanying actions did not seem to be important to him as though the journey itself was not very much in his thoughts.' 2. 'He seemed interested in choosing two dolls of contrasting size. He seemed keen to move the smaller one away from the larger.'

(This observer is attempting to identify the objective level of abstraction, the objective meaning.)

Unintelligent observer's comments: 1. 'He chose two dolls, not the nicest by any means. He couldn't even think up names for them.' (This observer misses the point because he is not looking for the child's meaning) 2. 'He played as the babies' mother, dressing one of them to go on a train journey.' (This observer thinks at a PLOT level) 3. 'He didn't bother to use any of the garments lying round as a coat; he didn't make any train noises or anything to really make a train.' (This observer is looking at imitation skills.)

The Mother's comment: 'He is jealous of the new baby.'

(The mother is able to observe the *subjective* level of abstraction.)

Let us now look at some of the illustrations used earlier when we were discussing external action. How do they fit into the more complete model of internal/external action? In the instance of the child in the garden playing at cooking, we have assumed that the driving force has been a zeal for imitating the process of jelly- and trifle-making, or in a form of objective abstraction such as filling and emptying vessels of water. But in fact the principal motivation may be much more generalised: 'being the boss', 'being busy', 'being important', 'being creative'.

Supposing it is the first, 'being the boss', then he will inevitably adopt an attitude. He cannot remain neutral about 'being the boss', he must give the concept a value, so his feelings will guide him to 'it's fun to be a boss' or 'it's worrying' or 'it's satisfying' or 'overwhelming' or 'confusing' or 'rewarding', etc. In fact, an attitude can lie at any point or mixture of points along a positive–negative continuum from an extreme of pleasantness to an extreme of unpleasantness.

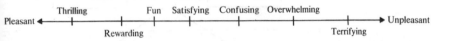

Let us assume that this child's attitude is that 'it's fun to be boss'. If this is the prime motivating factor then the *form* the play takes is a particularisation of the more general concept: the cooking fulfils this need, as later does the bathing and dressing the baby. It is interesting to note that if the urge to 'be the boss' is intense, this could correspondingly reduce the desire to create the cooking and baby contexts with any objectivity. Compare the dressing doll actions of a child whose underlying attitude is 'I want to be like Mother and do exactly as she does' with those of our child who simply 'wants to be in charge of things – anything!' The former would be bound to work at the level of objective abstraction, using imitative make-believe skill to a high degree. The latter will simply give a token representation of the real actions, making them no more than a reference point. Diagrammatically the two children's play might be shown like this:

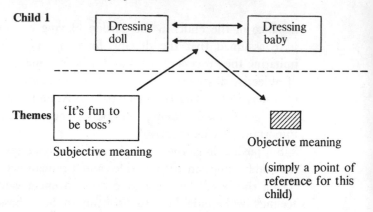

Note the congruence between the subjective and objective meanings in child no. 2.

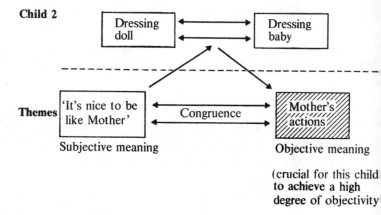

It is interesting to note the difference in treatment the same group of young children can give to the 'objective' meaning. I watched a group of children where 'being like adults' at a tea-party caused them to go through a very precise ritual of pouring, sugaring, stirring and sipping. The very next day when their drama work culminated with a feast celebrating their triumph over a monster, the gesture they used for eating was a token guiding of closed fingers to the mouth, their *minds* were far removed from objective attention to the details of eating procedures. It is worth commenting that a teacher given to Type C, theatre, as described in Chapter 1, often finds it very difficult to tolerate the latter kind of token gesture because a Type C teacher's major concern has to be 'How far does what the child is doing represent the *objective* world so that anyone watching would recognise it?' At the other extreme, it is possible to find Type B: dramatic playing teachers whose high degree of tolerance for *non-objective* treatment encourages, by default, the development in his pupils of the habit of wallowing in meaningless playing, a habit which can become as restricting as the most rigid theatre form.

All my sympathies go to the many teachers trained in Type C who, having been told that dramatic playing is educational, force themselves to relinquish their hold on the objective skills they could have passed on to their pupils in the name of free expression lose their integrity and their sanity. It is hoped that this book will help all teachers, of whatever background and training, to use their strengths.

But, I am anticipating . . . chapter 4 will have to be another theoretical excursion!

Questions

1 The author seems to claim a significant connection between child play and drama. Do you agree with him?
2 What would you suggest are the *differences* between play and drama?
3 To what extent do you feel it is a teacher's responsibility to interpret and to take into account secondary symbolism?

4 Learning in make-believe play and drama

When I was a young teacher colleagues might out of interest have asked me occasionally what I was doing with a particular class of children in drama, but nobody as far as I can remember actually asked me what I was *teaching* them; and I would have felt some personal insult if the question had been re-phrased to 'What actually are they *learning*?' Apparently learning and teaching were all right for other subjects, but in drama one just thought and talked about what one was *doing*.

Only in recent years, with publications such as John Fines' and Ray Verrier's *The History of Drama* (1974), Chris Day's *Drama in the Upper and Middle School* (1975), John O'Toole's *Theatre in Education* (1976), the Schools Council Secondary Drama Project *Learning Through Drama* (1977) and the Inner London Education Authority's *Drama Guidelines* (1977), have teachers been encouraged to think in terms of learning and teaching. Other publications have given us impressive lists of long-term aims such as developing the whole person, or inspiring confidence, or training the imagination, or giving social awareness. Few theorists and practitioners equipped teachers with the means of articulating answers to the question, 'What are you teaching these children now and what are they actually learning?'

This chapter will attempt to define the kinds of learning that are possible through drama, and again we turn to our model of external/internal action in make-believe play.

Let us look at our second hypothetical doll-playing child. For convenience let us turn her into a four-year-old girl. From the diagram of external action on page 23 it will be seen that there are two potential areas of change, the area of skills and the area of knowledge. In skills she may improve in manipulating the doll's clothes and she may become more

30

proficient at imitating her mother. In terms of knowledge she may have a variety of sensorimotor experiences or, at an internal level, newly appreciate the complexities of a mother's actions.

Now let us go back to our first child, our four-year-old boy, who also plays with his doll but with a very different motive. Supposing our 'it's fun to be boss' boy is joined by our 'it's nice to be like mother' girl for the ostensible purpose of sharing their doll play. If they interact at all there is bound to be a collision of attitudes. Not only are their subjective themes different but their objective priorities are just not compatible. If the boy is the stronger personality, the girl's sense of accuracy in imitating mother is going to be violated; if the girl is the stronger personality, the boy will have to adapt his attitude to meet the different concept of dressing the baby. Whichever way it goes, either or both of the children are in for a painful experience, a painful LEARNING EXPERIENCE.

We have now reached the main point of establishing the model of make-believe play. In play and in drama there is obvious learning potential in terms of skills and objective knowledge, but the deepest kind of change that can take place is at the level of subjective meaning. The learning does not have to be painful, as in the illustration, although it sometimes is and, in any case, it has to be *felt* for it to be effective.

It is this essential FEELING level that is often either not recognised or ignored by teachers. Others are aware of where they should be aiming but have no skills to get there, a few seem to be able to reach there intuitively. A recent article by Mrs B.J. Wagner on Dorothy Heathcote's teaching uses the phrase as her title 'evoking gut-level drama' (1974) as a way of encapsulating Mrs Heathcote's philosophy of teaching, but perhaps 'gut-level' is too dramatic a phrase, giving the impression as it does of traumatic change: Dorothy Heathcote's teaching is the best example we have of drama work operating at the level of subjective meaning but she does not require that it be sensational. Indeed, I was listening to her the other day, working with some teachers on various forms of planning for drama; they were discussing how to use drama to help: (*a*) a class of adolescents who were 'turned off' reading literature; and (*b*) another group who in their vocational guidance outings visited factories without really *seeing* anything. In each case drama could only be effective if the adolescents were touched emotionally enough to bring about a change of attitude, a change in the value they give either to reading or factory visits; in other words the teachers would have to work at the 'subjective meaning' level. That does not imply a spectacular, dramatic experience, but it does imply very careful planning by the teacher, something we shall be looking at later on.

A feature of Type D drama then is that it is primarily concerned with learning at a subjective level of meaning. To leave it like that, however, is misleading, as worthwhile change at a subjective level can only be brought about in terms of the objective. Let us see how our model works out when we look, not at child play, but at a drama experience. We have seen how complicated our over-simplication of just two children playing is, so we cannot anticipate an easy ride through the complexities of a group drama experience.

Our model is not yet detailed enough fully to discuss learning in drama, as a particular aspect of subjective meaning still has to be identified. We must therefore leave the concept of learning temporarily and attempt to break down 'subjective meaning' further. In so doing we shall begin to make a distinction between drama and play or, in behavioural terms, between what a child is doing when he is 'playing' compared with what he is doing when he is using the art form of drama.

I am trying to use my words carefully. I am not talking about creating an art. What is created may be good or bad art. At this stage I am only concerned with whether or not it is good education. I am suggesting that child play can undergo a 'change of gear' that gives it a dramatic art form. Children in their playing may accidentally or consciously move into this change of gear which we can call drama. In school drama children may slip out of gear back into playing unless the teacher has a firm hold on the gear lever.

Whereas it may seem inappropriate to make a value judgement of child play, to say 'that is good playing' or 'that is not so good', it is not unreasonable to make such a judgement in terms of educational drama. In that context therefore, I may use 'playing' as a pejorative description of an activity that is inferior to drama.

I am concerned here to draw a distinction between the two apparently similar activities. That distinction is centred on the quality of the subjective meaning within the activity. In drama and group playing it is necessary to recognise three different levels or aspects of that meaning:

1 Collective attitude congruent with objective meaning.
2 Personal feelings relevant to objective meaning.
3 Personal feelings irrelevant to objective meaning.

Working backwards, number 3 of this list is an individual attitude which only reveals itself when it becomes abnormal in some way.

Level 3

Examples of personal feelings irrelevant to objective meaning
(*a*) 'I hate drama.'
(*b*) 'I am going to show off my acting skills for the visitor.'
(*c*) 'I'm scared the teacher will chastise me if I don't do it right.'
(*d*) 'It's my birthday today.'
(*e*) 'I dislike being in this class.'
(*f*) 'I'm going to make the rest of the class laugh.'
(*g*) 'I'm hungry.'
(*h*) 'She doesn't play fairly.'
(*i*) 'I'm going to thump these kids.'

Let us now look at the next level dealing with personal but relevant feelings and in order to discuss relevance let us assume that the above illustrations represent some of the irrelevant feelings shared by a particular class of children involved in a particular drama experience. If any one of those feelings is strong enough it may mean that child is excluded from the make-believe activity at *any* level: he is in neither drama nor play.

Level 2

Personal feelings relevant to objective meaning
This refers to current or easily accessible feelings directly related to the make-believe context. Examples of such feelings of individual children might be:

(*a*) 'I fancy myself dressed in armour' – a lad playing a medieval knight.

(*b*) 'I'm scared of the dark' – the play is about the haunted house and teacher has just put the light off.

(*c*) 'I'm good at morse-code' – the play is about a shipwreck.

(*d*) 'Colin Green'll hit me at play-time if I don't tell him where the loot is' – the army officer forces his men to own up about the 'loot'.

(*e*) 'I'm scared of water' – the play is about a shipwreck.

(*f*) 'My dog died last week' – the play is about a king's funeral.

Levels 3 and 2, both consist of what Robert Witkin would call 'raw emotion', that is actual emotions felt by the children, varying in degrees to which they are relevant or irrelevant, extrinsic or intrinsic, lasting or spontaneous, already present or recalled, direct or oblique.

A closer look at level 3, however, will reveal that in certain circumstances some apparently irrelevant attitudes could become relevant. Supposing for example the child at 3(*e*) whose attitude is 'I dislike being in this class' becomes absorbed in the make-believe in a way that allows him, unconsciously, to express that attitude. He might for instance find himself volunteering to give up his place on the lifeboat in the classic drama situation: in other words he is manipulating the situation just as Piaget's jealous child does in sending the smaller doll on a journey.

Turning to look in some detail at the possibilities of the boy named Colin Green, referred to by our child at 2(*d*), let us assume that Colin Green is the child whose starting attitude was 3(*i*) 'I'm going to thump these kids'. Now if he carries that out, actually thumping other children, he is making no concession to the make-believe at all and is neither playing nor dramatising. But if, for the sake of the make-believe, Colin Green, who normally would not hesitate about punching a few ribs, actually restrains himself and only 'pretends to punch', it has to be argued that he is playing. This is fine if he is supposed to be playing an officer demanding to know where the loot is – his natural bullying inclination fits – but if the drama was to do with the delights of having a summer's day picnic, his pretending to bully people could seem out of place. Now this kind of incongruence may be a common feature of play but it seems to me it cannot be acceptable in drama. In such circumstances therefore you could say that whereas the rest of the class was doing drama, Colin Green was 'merely' playing. On the other hand if he takes the rest of the class along with him, or the teacher helps the others to see the positive possibilities in a play about a picnic undermined by the presence of a bully it could be said that they have moved towards drama again. I am deliberately using *towards* as it seems to be a matter of orientation rather than classification.

If the class as a whole is working at level 1 of 'subjective' meaning then there is certainly a drama orientation.

Level 1

Collective attitude congruent with objective meaning
Activity at this level is dependent on the class having identified what it is that interests them in the make-believe topic – what they propose to *abstract* from that topic. If, for instance, the title of their drama is 'Space-ship' what are some of the possibilities? (If they were in Type B, Dramatic playing, they would whip up a fast sequence of dramatic adventures; if they were in Type C, Theatre, they might build up a powerful story-line.) Aspects of 'space-ship' abstractions might be:

Going into the unknown
Expertise required of crew
Qualities of a captain
Complexity of machinery
Planning for emergencies
Keeping communications going
Looking after one's own body
Welfare of passengers.

Now at the subjective meaning level 1 the participants must find attitudes, feeling qualities that are appropriate for any *one* of the above (any one at a time that is.) The drama that starts with applicants proving their worth as crew members, may move to a focus on 'keeping communications going' or an overpowering sense of 'going into the unknown'; the important point is that each of these abstractions must be focused on by the whole group at the same time for the experience to be drama rather than playing.

The feeling qualities evoked to match the objective meaning of 'going into the unknown' might within a class vary from 'it is alarming' to 'it is exhilarating'; for 'the complexity of machinery' they might range along 'we cannot/must not/will not/dare not make mistakes'; in concern for 'the welfare of the passengers' the feeling might be 'this responsibility is alarming/challenging/too much/well within our powers'. Whichever attitude is adopted it must be *felt*, not pretended if a child is to experience working at level 3 of subjective meaning. We are now in a position to distinguish four features giving the activity a drama orientation, (1) sharing; (2) congruency; (3) ascendancy over the personal level of subjectivity; and (4) a feeling quality that is not the raw emotion of daily living.

1. *Sharing.* This point has already been made clear, that the members of the group collectively identify with a selected focus of the make-believe.

2. *Congruency.* The feeling qualities must match the objective meaning. A further explanation is necessary here. The feeling is an *appraisal* of the objective situation and therefore congruence implies a compatibility between a child's feeling

about and understanding of a situation. Congruence is not a linking with some adult's concept of the situation. Suppose, for instance, a group of Protestant children in Northern Ireland, brought up to believe that Catholics are the enemy, enact a drama about Belfast with the underlying subjective attitude that Catholics are both stupid and wicked: in so far as that is their genuine perception of the situation the subjective and objective meanings could be described as congruent. An example of incongruence would be where in a 'shipwreck' play the attitude displayed was 'it's fun to jump for the lifeboats' where the participants' own intellectual grasp of the situation has taught them that, objectively, this is just not the case. Such an example would be 'playing' in a pejorative sense – an orientation away from drama.

3. *Ascendancy of the collective over the personal level of subjectivity.* We have seen from earlier examples that if the personal level dominates for any particular child, unless he submits to other factors (sharing, congruence and feeling modification), he will either be playing or be outside the rules of play altogether. Ascendancy must be seen as a matter of balance for the personal level does not disappear: indeed it is the main source of energy.

4. *A feeling quality.* Susanne Langer, in *Philosophy in a New Key* (1963), asserts, 'Sheer self-expression requires no artistic form' (p. 216). The feelings at levels 2 and 3 are, it seems to me, of that order, the 'raw emotion' of self-expression. In level 1 there is a modifying of spontaneous feeling; a feeling quality is achieved that is either readily accessible (as in the case of the natural bully who draws on his conception of bullying but who subsequently simulates the real action) or recalled from specific past experience (as in the case of a child in the shipwreck episode who is scared of water) or recalled – and this is the most common source – from a more general matrix of feeling experience (a child, for example, who has no experience of death can find a quality of sadness or grief or regret, etc., drawn from different personal experiences, including imagining death, that allows him to participate in the play about the king's death). This 'filtering' of feeling does not imply either a reduction of

emotion or a falsification of emotion. It is different in quality.

To summarise, subjective meaning is dependent on the interaction of three levels. The level that moves the experience towards drama, the collective level, is characterised by its special quality of feeling, its sharing, its ascendancy over personal levels and its congruence with objective meaning. It is at this level that the most important kind of learning takes place in Type D drama. The learning is concerned with a change in the relationship between the collective subjective meaning and the objective meaning. In case the reader feels that by definition subjective meaning cannot be collective, let me put it another way: it is a change in the value given to a situation or concept, a change in appraisal, the affective aspect of which appears to be sufficiently shared by members of the group for it to provide a common reference point.

At last we have reached the central point of this book: that drama in education is primarily concerned with change in appraisal, an affective/cognitive development. We can conveniently refer to it as 'Drama for understanding': this is what the teacher is teaching and the learner is learning. We shall be examining this 'learning area' in different ways in subsequent chapters. It will suffice here to give a few illustrations to clarify the kind of concept with which we are most concerned.

Because drama operates subjectively and objectively the learning is related to those concepts about which value judgements are made. The kind of important learning that deliberately discourages value judgements (for example, the classification of animals into vertebrates and non-vertebrates) is best acquired, in my opinion, through modes other than drama. On the other hand a concept such as 'Progress relies on people taking risks' might be understood differently if the learner is subjected to the experiential mode of drama. Most concepts can have both kinds of orientation. Take the concept of 'protection': an evolutionist or a zoologist may examine different ways in which animals do or do not protect their young; a sociologist may similarly research protection of one generation by another among human beings. But 'protection' as a concept can also connote a whole range of personal meanings that stem from the user's affective life. It is these meanings that drama can most carefully open up for the participants. As educationalists we have failed to appreciate this dual orientation. We have assumed that pedagogy is the training of children in the neutral observation of objective facts. Teachers have often only paid lip-service to, or ignored, the affective orientation or, equally mistakenly, have assumed that such an orientation means free expression rather than understanding. In my view, both orientations are directed towards the development of concepts and we have a responsibility to make both modes available to the children we teach. Not only do we neglect the affective orientation but often train our children to despise it. The teacher of history feels it incumbent on him to teach the fact that Edward the Confessor left the matter of succession to the throne vague, but not to open up for his pupils the emotional ambivalence of making or interpreting a half-promise (I am grateful to Ray Verrier for this illustration); the geography teacher may teach the fact that the Banaban people were evacuated from their Pacific Island home so that the British government might continue to destroy it for phosphate quarrying, but he does not see it as part of his job to explore the nature of that people's distress. Perhaps the saddest examples I could give of this single orientation are to be drawn from the teaching of English literature, where so many teachers seem to avoid giving their pupils an emotional understanding but train them instead to intellectualise about emotions: they can recite how Lady Macbeth felt when she read her husband's letter but they do not *know* how she felt. That is something many English teachers fail to tap. If a child in his class does not understand a word, his English teacher may willingly fish around for the equivalent words the child does know so that a bridging between the known and the new can take place. But if the emotional experience within the literature is unfamiliar to the child he will not necessarily consider it part of his job to find out where the child is emotionally in order to make that particular bridge. So the child is denied the affective experience.

There are two important consequences of this limited form

of education. What is intellectually understood is rarely enriched by subjective understanding, and, more importantly, the objective world of the child grows apace so that as he gets older he has more and more sophisticated objective measures to draw upon, but his education has deliberately avoided extending his range and sophistication of feeling so that all he has to draw on in this respect are those emotional experiences he happens to meet. Many teachers who are shocked at the negative emotional responses of their pupils do not realise that feeling, like intellect, is something that can be improved in quality and that both are a teacher's responsibility.

Questions

1 Do you agree with the points made in the final paragraph of this chapter?
2 The author has now attempted to distinguish between play and drama. Are his arguments helpful?
3 If you were working with a class on the topic of 'cave-man' what aspects might you usefully abstract?

5 Some implications of drama for understanding

In Chapter 4 I have tried to establish that learning in Type D drama is concerned with a change of insight. To theatre-minded teachers reading this text let me make it clear that I am not talking about 'characters' who undergo change, but the pupils themselves. For drama to be effective in these terms there must be some shift of appraisal, an act of cognition that has involved a change of feeling, so that some facet of living is given (however temporarily) a different value.

Let us give examples from actual drama experiences of this kind of change.

Type of class	Starting attitude	Final attitude as a direct result of drama
Aged 17+ mixed	It is expedient to lie to protect ourselves.	Doubts on long-term value of the lie.
Aged 12+ sub-normal	Police are 'the enemy'.	A policeman is a man with a home and a family.
Aged 11+ mixed	We trust this leader without question.	We should have questioned!
Aged 9+	Problems have black or white solutions.	Some problems seem unresolvable.
Aged 7+	Obstacles can be overcome simply by changing the rules.	Obstacles can be overcome even without changing the rules— if you work hard enough.
Aged 6+ mixed	Africans are primitive and quaint.	Africans are like us in many ways.

Adults	We are concerned with the problem of the old lady.	We are concerned with what that problem does to *us*.
Aged 6+	'Solutions' are easily found.	'Solutions' have consequences.

I hope readers have looked at this table with a healthy suspicion. There is an implication that members of the classes listed in the left-hand column, having all started with the attitude listed in the middle column, in the process of the drama lesson or lessons (the table gives no indication of the length of time employed), obligingly move over to the attitudes listed in the third column. Such a notion is, of course, nonsense. Although the table does represent particular past lessons of mine, all I can claim is that in some instances, some children appeared to move (during some part of the experience) in the direction of the new attitudes or awarenesses.

The 'success' in these terms was spectacular in the case of the eleven-year-olds who having, in their play, joined a gang to rob Fort Knox, found out at the eleventh hour that their leader (the teacher) was getting cold feet over the whole thing. Their anger and frustration was intense. It took no subtlety of observation on my part to assess that they regretted having trusted him in the first place. On the other hand I have no illusions that a group of twelve-year-old boys who clearly regarded the police as enemies (most of them and their parents, in fact, had recently been in police hands) were likely to have undergone a miraculous attitude change as a result of the drama experience. That *some* boys however for the first time glimpsed the possibility of a policeman being a person is a way of edging towards breaking their original stereotype. It is just a drop on a stone and to the extent that the drama experience squeezed out that drop it could be regarded as effective drama.

There is some confusion in the way the middle column describes the attitudes. Sometimes they appear to belong to the participants themselves (e.g. obstacles can be overcome simply by changing the rules) but other examples are clearly referring to the attitude 'in role' (e.g. we are concerned with the problem of the old lady). The confusion arises because some groups (particularly adolescents and adults) will only reveal their true attitudes by the way they set up a role. It is not as I have said above, the attitude of the 'character' that the teacher is concerned with but the participant's perception of that role. If, for example, I observe that adolescents, in setting up their drama about a psychiatric hospital, begin to role-play patients as people with crazy, irrational, antisocial behaviour, I would probably go along with this extreme stereotyping, initially. The 'patients' may gradually undergo change but what I as teacher would really be concerned with is the underlying attitude and understanding that caused these adolescents to choose: (*a*) that particular topic, and (*b*) that extreme version of the topic. It is only when you know the *feeling* behind the choice that you as teacher have any real chance of knowing what can best be learnt. On the other hand attitudes are sometimes made explicit before any drama starts: 'History's daft' puts a teacher very clearly in the picture!

At the other extreme from this explicitness it sometimes (often?) happens that a teacher for part or all of the work simply has no idea of what is being learnt. He has not in his mind been able to detect and define a starting attitude about anything in particular; the direction in which the children are taking the drama is not giving him any clues. What the teacher does about this will be dealt with in a later chapter. The point to be established here is that important as it is for the teacher to define the change in understanding it may not always be possible to do so for the variety of reasons discussed since I set out that concise but misleading attitude table.

Nevertheless, that I still set it out while recognising its deficiencies is perhaps another indication of the importance I place on this kind of learning. It seems useful to identify four possible stages in such learning during a drama experience.

Four stages towards change in understanding

Stage 1: artificial drama
This applies to what I like to refer to as 'artificial' drama where the feeling quality brought to the experience by the participants is not compatible with their intellectual understanding of the subject matter.

I recall working with a class of twelve-year-olds on a drama about 'The Plague of London'. The lesson took place in a large school hall with an impeccably polished floor. To my horror, dying of the plague became a huge adventure because of the physical delight of having your dead body whipped at speed along the shiny surface, deposited at the far corner of the hall and then, given a reasonable length of time and reassurance that teacher hadn't spotted you, a resurrection took place so that you could die and be dragged across the floor all over again. That is 'artificial' drama!

But the artificiality is often more subtle. An example is often found on teachers' drama courses where they enact stories suitable for the age group of children they normally teach without attempting to find a universal truth within the story that could be relevant to their adult selves. Adults too often avoid finding any appropriate feeling by hiding behind excessive verbalisation so that they are virtually holding a discussion and are not in drama at all.

Another kind of artificiality is from children who are trained to imitate emotion – a demonstration of weeping in grief where the only feeling is one of pleasure at simulating grief. And a very common kind of artificial drama is where children are allowed to 'play-out' freely in their own way and where their sole objective is really to have fun, irrespective of the subject matter they are enacting.

None of these activities can lead to change in understanding as there is no congruence between feeling and objectivity.

Stage 2: reinforcement
In order to create their drama participants can draw only on what they already know: unless some factor brings about

change the drama remains an unconscious reiteration of what is already understood. Much acting out of stories at a 'what happened next' level falls into this category. Although an improvement on the artificial level, its educational value is doubtful.

Stage 3: clarification

Type A, exercise drama, often leads to greater clarification which may take place during the planning of the exercise, the subsequent action reinforcing the concepts just clarified, or during the enactment itself. The kind of drama popular in our secondary schools where children are split into small groups to work at some topic, say a social problem, invites this kind of learning. Often the enactment is a kind of demonstration of whatever ideas they have clarified in their pre-discussion rather than a living-through, insightful experience. Adolescents often feel safe with this kind of drama as it allows their feelings to remain unexposed, but sometimes they and their teachers mistake it for the real thing. Nevertheless it has educational value, for clarification is in itself an important kind of modification. Often a child is helped to grasp some value that hitherto he has held implicitly: 'making the implicit explicit' has long been recognised as a significant function of drama.

Stage 4: modification

Only when the work is at an experiential feeling level can change in understanding take place. The modification can take many forms, some of which have already been touched on. Various metaphorical terms are used in an attempt to describe the insightful change that can take place: refining, extending, widening, making more flexible, shifting a bias, breaking a stereotype, giving new slant, challenging, casting doubt, questioning assumptions, facing decisions, seeing new implications, anticipating consequences, trying alternatives, widening range of choice, changing perspective.

Vague as this terminology is and intangible as the results may be in research terms, I claim that it is the most significant form of learning directly attributable to drama experience. Having this as a priority affects all my subsequent thinking about drama: the selection of goals, the selection of strategies, the assessment of results, and the way I defend the subject to other educationists, to head teachers and to parents.

Does this imply that if you were to see me teaching drama you would be bound to witness a deft manipulation by me of the pupils' understanding at some impressive 'feeling' level? Certainly not! Having one's priorities clear and being able to achieve them are two painfully different things! (See Ch. 8 and 9 for an analysis of priorities.) I have suggested there are four discernible stages in the work. Even the best teachers can find themselves struggling unsuccessfully with 'artificial' drama – for a variety of reasons. (I still recall with a distinct sting of embarrassment, allowing a class of infant children to run so wild that not a single serious thought passed through their heads during a whole lesson – and the next lesson too.)

The three qualities of learning I have discerned (reinforcement, clarification and modification) could almost be regarded as *fused stages* necessary to most drama work, except that the flow is normally a forward and backward movement; even a regressing from modification to artificial is possible. Diagrammatically it looks like this:

ARTIFICIAL ⇌ REINFORCING ⇌ CLARIFYING ⇌ MODIFYING

(Brian Watkins [1974] has gone into this notion of a lesson flow chart more thoroughly.) Let me reiterate that many educationally worthwhile drama lessons never reach the final stage. Indeed it is possible that a lesson that never gets beyond the artificial could be worthwhile in terms *other than conceptual*. Imagine the following sets of circumstances:

1 A mixed class of secondary children, dramatically creating something that is trivial, undemanding and far below what they are intellectually capable of. But suppose that in order to set up their childish material the boys and girls in the class co-operated for the first time.

46

2 The school has been on exams all week and the adolescents want to use the drama lesson 'just to have fun'.
3 A child in the class who is normally destructive of other people's work for once shows some signs of commitment, what he actually does is phony but for him it represents progress.
4 A group of adolescent girls, embarrassed by the topic they have chosen to dramatise, abortion, treat it in a casual, silly way: they are revealing to each other, in the only way that seems available, their very real concern.

It seems to me that the best possible judgement a teacher might make in any one of the above four circumstances (and I am sure the reader can think of more such instances) is to leave well alone. A good teacher will know what might have been done with the material given better circumstances, and will know exactly why he is leaving it alone in spite of recognising the potential dangers in so doing. The weak or inexperienced teacher's judgement may have the same outcome but will not be made as a result of balancing a complexity of priorities. Rarely are decisions in drama unidimensional; just as a parent may have to decide between breaking a promise to take a young daughter swimming and risking that an incipient cough might be made worse, so a drama teacher judges between, say, allowing a class to 'let off steam' and demanding serious commitment. The teacher of the adolescent girls must respect the girls' feelings and yet be aware that in so doing he risks failing to teach them that such trivialisation provides a false protection too easily donned.

An illustration

It may help the reader at this point if I try to apply the preceding theoretical structure to an instance of actual teaching, taking the example of six-year-olds doing their drama about Africans.

The children were intelligent, white, middle-class Californians who, under the guidance of a very talented teacher in an open-plan school, had been doing a project on primitive and modern Africa for a period of four weeks. They were well informed on many African customs to do with agriculture, houses, music and dances, but the teacher felt that in spite of their intellectual grasp of the project the children's general attitude towards the Africans was that they were quaint and inferior. She invited me to use drama to try to bring about a broader view. I worked with them for an hour a day for five days.

You will recall that an earlier example of the artificial level of drama was when children relished the idea of dying of the plague. These six-year-old children in role-playing a primitive tribe of Africans at times displayed a similar superficial level, when their high degree of emotional investment had nothing whatsoever to do with the symbolic situation. There were moments in the first two days when the physical novelty of the environment was in itself of over-riding interest. For instance, when they were allowed to use tables as huts, sitting under them out of sight of teacher had its own attractions. For a few children the opportunity and challenge of climbing on to a cupboard in order to 'break a high branch from the tall tree' was irresistible; for others the scramble to have a chance to 'play the drum' had nothing to do with the drum as the sole means of communication to the distant village.

But these distracting moments were rare in this particular sequence of lessons. Initially a great deal of time was spent putting into action what they already knew about African customs, in other words a reinforcing stage that allowed them to go through 'quaint' motions of miming cleaning their teeth with a special bark or cooking 'fou-fou' – all very charming but quite undemanding. I felt that one possible way of helping these children to find real human qualities in Africans was (*a*) to reveal that they (the Africans) in their way were as skilled as Americans, and (*b*) to show that the two nations had important things in common. I imposed therefore a plot situation of a cry for help from a village, three days away, that needed our help to trap a marauding lion. This would look after (*a*) above in terms of skills, stamina, patience and careful planning, and also (*b*) in that it would feed in an attitude to home. The business of leaving one's home and returning to it is a matter of some concern to six-year-old Americans – and, so it seemed from the drama, to Africans too. I structured heavily the preparations for leaving and the moment of parting from our huts – for two whole lessons in fact.

This was in the main a clarification stage where the class was constantly being asked to sort out its priorities in journey preparations and practise skills appropriate for trapping the lion. The children drew heavily and, in the excitement of the drama, desperately, on all they thought they might know or not know about preparation for urgent future events. The intellectual demands were high (typically so of a clarification phase).

What they finally experienced, broadly speaking, was a triumph of success: all their hard work bore fruit; they captured the lion with an enormous effort of co-operative group discipline. They returned to their homes as victors. They had the pride shared by everyone at a job well done. And the next day when they came across a stranger (the teacher in role) from somewhere called America, a stranger who talked of 'quaint' things like jeeps and refrigerators and telephones, they stood up with him as equals, if not superiors, explaining as best they could to someone who was not likely to understand the nature of their triumphs. And when this stranger said America was offering them money to use on their choice between roads, jeeps, guns or toys, they voted finally for toys. When asked 'Why toys?' one girl replied: 'You can tell the Americans that we love our children too.'

For at least one child the concept of Africans had been filled out a bit. This is an example of what I mean by drama as a medium for *learning*. Rarely will what has been learnt be stated so explicitly. Many times as teacher you will not be sure whether that level has been reached for enough of the children in the class. Many more times you will be disappointed that it has not been reached at all. Fortunately other goals – clarification, social co-operation, communication skills, etc. – are important educational ends in themselves.

Questions

1 From your own drama experience are you able to identify any one or more of the four stages?
2 What do you consider you have learnt from past drama experiences? Discuss one in detail.

6 Dramatic structure – exercise

In Chapter 5 we looked at four stages of learning in dramatic activity: a preparatory stage not conductive to learning (artificial stage); a stage concerned with unconscious reiteration of what is familiar (reinforcement); a conscious identifying of what is known (clarification); and a shift of perspective (modification).

This notion of learning is very much a teacher's, not his pupils', view of dramatic activity. Indeed Geoffrey Gillham (1974) has usefully drawn a distinction between 'the play for the teacher' and 'the play for the children'. In other words, when children and teacher work together on drama there are virtually two complementary plays: the children's with its 'what happens next' orientation and the teacher's with its educational goals. The degree to which a teacher modifies their 'play' will depend not merely on his ability to do so, but more importantly on the philosophical position he takes as a teacher of drama. This book is written on the assumption that the teacher has a responsibility to work towards goals which reach beyond and above the children's. But he cannot do this without respect for their intentions. It is a delicate balance. I recall reading an article somewhere with the title, 'Starting from where the children are at . . . and leaving them there!' If the final balance between the two is not achieved the children will certainly be left where they started, either because 'the play for them' has predominated or because the teacher has bounded ahead with his play to the entire neglect of theirs.

Geoffrey Gillham saw this distinction between the two plays in terms of respective intentions or *goals*, but it can also usefully be drawn in terms of the respective *structures* of the two plays. This brings us full circle back to Chapter 1, where I argued that there are three main orientations in dramatic activity. Type A, Exercise; covers many kinds of activity but tends to be characterised by a sense of purpose, clarity of outline, repeatability and defined rules. Type B, Dramatic playing, appears to be the converse of Type A, in that its existential mode has less circumscribed features. Type C, Theatre, differs from the other two in its emphasis on communication of an end-product to an audience.

A fourth type of drama it was claimed in Chapter 1 was somehow dependent upon a combination of these three. If we look again at the 'African' illustration this time in terms of its structures we will see how a combination of these three orientations can operate within the same dramatic activity.

In one sense the whole occasion was five hours of dramatic playing in that the children were in role for most of that time and the outcome was apparently open-ended. To a visitor casually glancing in from time to time it might look like a whole class of twenty-five children playing at being Africans. But such is the peculiar structure of Type D drama that it can have the appearance of loose dramatic playing; indeed its basic element of 'living through' in a moment-to-moment experience is crucial, but this is combined with the purposefulness, the economy and the tautness of a good dramatic exercise.

If we look at the African sequence as a series of sections, the list appears as follows:

'Let's work out how big the raft will have to be if it is to carry all of us.'

'Do you think singing a song will help our weariness?'

'Search in the forests for the right kind of fibre and report to your head of family what you have found and where you have found it.'

'Who has been told the past brave deeds of our tribe? Can you tell us what you know?'

'This is a day that none of us will forget. As we sit round the dying embers, let every man and woman say what is in their mind.'

'Who can show the rest of us how best to sharpen our spears?'

'Let us work out step by step, what the best tactics are for trapping that lion.'

'Now that we have decided how to go about it, could we have a practice so that we find out what the snags might be?'

'What are the different messages that can be conveyed by drum-beat to the old man left behind?'

Isolated in this way, items in the above list stand out clearly as exercises. They fit many of the criteria for Type A, Exercise, indicated in Chapter 1. For example:

Always short-term; often there is a sense of completion.
Always a specific goal.
Sometimes an answer to be found.
Always has a cutting-off point, when there is nothing to be gained by continuing, etc.

And yet this is *not* Type A drama for they are also *experiencing* an activity called 'Going on a journey to hunt a lion'. Thus exercise structures are, as it were, 'folded in' to the overall dramatic playing form. To put it another way, the exercise structure of the 'play for the teacher' is integrated with the existential living-through structure of 'the play for the children'.

We need, however, to probe further with this concept of a relationship between two structures. We first need to know more precisely what we mean by 'living-through'. Like all experiencing, 'living-through' has a double aspect: (*a*) a sense of 'it is happening to me', and (*b*) 'I am making it happen': the first is passive; the second active. When a baby is hugged by his mother, the experience is almost entirely passive; when he becomes his own agent and hugs his mother he has reduced the passivity in one way but retained it in another in that he must submit to the effect of his own activity on himself. Similarly when a child beats on a drum, he submits to the sound it makes. When a group of children play the game, 'What time is it, Mr Wolf?' they are their own agents: they have selected the game; they can stop it any time they wish; they are in control. And yet it would also be valid to say that they have contrived this situation so that they might be controlled by it. For indeed, unless they submit themselves to the experience of 'it is happening to us' they are failing to taste the game's excitement. 'They are not really experiencing it,' we might say. It is rather like a guest at a party who cannot let the party happen to him.

It is this ambivalent quality of controlling so that one might be controlled that is a central feature of child play. When Vygotsky's children play at being sisters they are controlling, 'making it happen'. But *it* must *happen* to *them* for them to have the experience. Vygotsky claims that children are made finely aware by their make-believe, but it seems to me that unless the two sisters in the process of their contriving also submit to the 'sister' experience that is created, there will be nothing for them to be finely aware of.

Significantly then all experience potentially has two functions. Perhaps certain kinds of clearly defined child play and games in particular make the distinction clear. In 'What time is it, Mr Wolf?', in so far as the participants are at work applying the rules of the game they are actively circumscribing experience, but in so far as they are subjecting themselves to the rules they are opening themselves up to spontaneous experience. The one function controls; the other releases.

If we now return to dramatic activity, it will be seen that dramatic playing has the same double function of controlling and being released. Whereas there is much dramatic playing that does not have as clearly defined a controlling aspect as in a game with rules or as in a precise form of playing like the Vygotsky example, the 'making it happen' function is nevertheless operating. When dramatic playing appears to be at its most free, the participants are contriving to set up rules to 'make things happen' even though collectively they might not agree on what they are. The other side of the coin, 'it is happening to us' is often there in large measure.

When we speak of dramatic playing structure we are really referring to the two complementary active and passive modes of functioning. It is the latter, 'it is happening to me now', that has the qualities we might describe as existential or living-through; the former on the other hand has qualities

54

of defining, controlling, contriving and anticipating. It is this active mode that is accessible to the teacher of Type D drama. When the teacher 'folds into' Type B Dramatic playing, a structure that belongs to Type A, Exercise, he is virtually extending the child's 'I am making it happen' mode, for the exercise form tends also to be characterised by its defining, controlling, contriving and anticipating qualities. (A glance at the list on p. 52 from the African sequence will verify this.) He has, however, taken the reins from the children's hands (for he is in 'the play for the teacher' with its educational goals). If the delicate balance referred to earlier is not achieved, there is a danger that he will have changed it to 'I, the teacher alone, am making it happen', rather than 'we, the teacher and class, are making it happen'.

And it should never happen in Type D drama that teacher with class can add 'it is happening to us' for the teacher does not belong to the living-through experience. He must never submit to the experience. His participation must always be from an exercise or, as we shall see later, a theatre structure. His function is to contrive, not to participate in the full dramatic-playing sense.

The instrumental function

It has been argued in the first part of this chapter that the characteristics of exercise in so far as they are defining and controlling tend to correspond with those qualities that distinguish the 'I am making it happen' mode of dramatic playing and of child play. Because they both share this instrumental function the teacher may employ exercises in the service of dramatic playing: what the teacher does is structurally an extension of what children themselves already do. We shall now examine what factors affect this instrumental function when it is handled by children alone and when a teacher sees fit to take it over.

The child as agent in the particularisation process
If the reader glances back at the diagram on p. 25 he will

be reminded that when a child plays there is a mixture of internal and external action. The external action is what is observable and reportable. In the particular instance quoted from Piaget the child might show or report 'I am Mummy and these are my children'. The external action represents the surface meaning of the experience; the internal action, on the other hand, represents the meaning that gave the principal impetus to the activity (in this case, jealousy of a sibling) and the ordering of the objective world in order to express or find the meaning he desires. In the instance Piaget described, the child was not conscious of this internal action.

The simplicity of this classic example is misleading: there must be many occasions when play is multi-motivated with a whole range of meanings none of which may have much significance for either the observer or for the child himself. Nevertheless, such an example can help us learn about structure. We can see from the diagram that make-believe play is a process of particularisation; whatever internal meaning motivates the play it can only be expressed in concrete action. There are at least two kinds of selecting going on: (1) the conscious choice of context (being Mother with children); and (2) abstracting those aspects of the context that are likely to create the required experience (different sized dolls and the action of moving one from the other). This twofold selection is part of the instrumental functioning of play.

Drama operates in the same way. Children who have been impressed by a visit to the fire station select that topic for their drama and within it make a further selection of specific actions that have qualities (speed, efficiency, daring, etc.) that allow them to have the experience they seek.

It sometimes happens in drama, however, that the selection process is unrealistic in terms of felt value or that each participant is enjoying his own play. The teacher is often required to take over the instrumental functioning and to extend it into exercise form so that shared identification with the topic at a serious level can take place.

The teacher as agent in the particularisation process
I have suggested that most drama in schools is not a group's
expression of some collective concern but more likely some
much milder form of commitment. Put another way, relating
to our earlier discussions, the feeling quality they initially
bring to their roles is not likely to be compatible with their
realistic understanding of the roles they play. So, for
example, children role-play prisoners or hijackers or hospital
nurses or school teachers or the people of Hamelin or the
women of Troy without *experiencing* these roles: the over-
riding feeling quality may be one of sheer pleasure at role-
playing prisoners or hijackers etc. Although we want the
pleasure of enactment to be retained, it cannot remain an
overriding feature; it must give way to feeling qualities
appropriate to the role.

If the list provided on p. 36 of what might be considered
appropriate attitudes for the role play in a 'space-ship'
adventure, represents a high degree of selection in two
directions, objective and subjective. The objective selection
breaks down 'space-ship' into quite different aspects: going
into the unknown, expertise required of crew, qualities of a
captain, complexity of machinery, etc. This selecting process
obviously narrows down the 'meaning' of the experience.
Whatever 'space-ship' variously meant to the participants
before the drama started and whatever new meanings
accrue over several hours work, the starting point is going to
be very limited. In fact they are, at least temporarily, in a
different play if the emphasis is placed on 'keeping communication going' rather than 'qualities of a captain'. This
limitation is necessary for three reasons: (1) the categorising
of meaning has a chance of linking the novel subject matter
with what the children already know: they may not know
much about space-ships but they will be able to draw on
some experience of communication lines or leadership etc.;
(2) it provides a shared experience: left to themselves a class
of children, as I have suggested before, may be participating
in six different plays, all under the umbrella heading of
'space-ship'; (3) dramatic form can only operate when there
is a particularisation. This latter point merits discussion in

57

some detail here.

Drama can only function when an actor (using the term broadly here to mean participant) uses himself in time and space (action) to evoke some meaning that is not present in actuality. However profound or complex the thought being expressed, it can only be revealed through an actor's particular action in a particular sequence of time. Drama is the most concrete art form: in this lies its power, and also its weakness if the actions are not significant, but more of that later.

So whatever the topic, a particularisation in action must be found. 'Space-ship' cannot be enacted; keeping open communications, although usefully narrowing the field of action, cannot be enacted; but fingers of the right hand on the radio switch marked 'ON' and 'OFF' can be enacted. If the children do not themselves find this kind of particularisation then the teacher must help them – in two ways. First, by making sure that the action is a shared experience, by all being involved in the same action ('Let us work out on this blackboard what kind of code we are going to use when we send messages'), or by separately but simultaneously being involved in the same action ('Let us each put the personal message we would like sent back to Earth on to our cassette recorders'), or by being involved vicariously as we all watch in silence as the radio officer's fingers turn the switch to 'ON'; secondly, by supplying an attitude.

It is not enough to select an appropriate action. That represents merely the objective aspect of the environment that cannot by itself have much educational significance. The teacher cannot content himself by thinking: Hospitals? Ah yes, making beds; Supermarkets? Ah yes, taking purchases from shelves; Casino? Ah yes, round roulette table; Factory? Ah yes, working machines. Such categorising misses out entirely the subjective direction that any actions must take.

We are back again on our 'feeling qualities'. If the teacher does not supply an underlying attitude to the action there will necessarily be one. It may vary from child to child or it may have been dictated by the natural leader of the class. It may be consciously chosen or the children may be unaware. There cannot be an action without a subjective meaning, that is, some relationship between the action and the child doing it. Again the teacher's concern is with the criterion of appropriateness. I recently worked with a group of adults who in simulating a '1920s cocktail party' immediately adopted tinsel-like small talk among people who were bored with each other. Superficial, but at least the action had started with a feeling quality that reasonably belongs to the chosen context. As teacher I found this acceptable and helped them build on this satisfactory starting point, on this initial 'meaning'. On the other hand I cannot accept the initial work of a group of adults who with serious faces but somewhat tongue-in-cheek became a primitive tribe 'busy' with their pot-making and weaving. The latter needed to find a more clearly defined attitude for their potentially useful action and belief in the make-believe to begin.

This process of defining an attitude needs close examination. I will continue with the primitive tribe illustration as this happens to be a useful extreme, in the sense that it is a context far removed from the actors' own lives. No actor can act a 'primitive tribesman' – it doesn't mean anything. He can, however, select an action that such a person might perform, such as making a coil pot, but this alone is not enough for the meaning still has to be defined. It is an attitude to the action that the actor must find. Only then does he have a chance of 'believing' in what he is doing. For instance, suppose the attitude he selects (or the teacher selects for him) is 'I am proud of my skill', the action with his hands takes on that particular meaning.

This new dimension has a double function: (1) it allows the actor to tap an aspect of life he already emotionally understands, and (2) the action now represents a more universal concept of 'people who are proud of their skills'. The test of validity for this action, therefore, is not the question, 'Is he a primitive tribesman?', to which there can be no answer, but 'Is he someone who is proud of his skills?' The action means 'pride in skill' carried out merely *in the name of* primitive tribesman. It is possible that as the drama proceeds the participants learn more and more about primitiveness;

on the other hand it may be that the entire drama experience is virtually about something else – for instance, the meaning of education explored within the context of a primitive tribe, where the comparative simplicity of the context highlights the essential nature of the subject matter. The success of this latter experience does not depend upon an extended knowledge of a primitive tribe. Thus, using our 'skills' illustration again, what began as an exercise in defining the action of making a pot, 'we are proud of our skills', turned as the drama proceeded into an examination of the concept of education and never became, as an end in itself, a study of a primitive society.

Thus when the teacher becomes the agent for starting the process of particularisation, he may have to help the class (1) find an angle within a topic, (2) select an action and (3) provide a value dimension relating to that action. Let us look at some examples from past lessons:

	Topic	Selected beginning action	Attitude
1	Northern Ireland (13 years)	Shopping in supermarket	Life must go on.
2	*The Pied Piper of Hamelin* (adults)	Waiting at home for the lost children to return	We must talk about ordinary things.
3	Robbing a bank (10 years)	Arriving at a planning meeting	We must not draw attention to ourselves
4	Scouts (12 years)	Fixing tents	We must please scoutmaster.
5	Prison camp (14 years)	Playing a ball game	We must fight the boredom.
6	Monster (6 years)	Going to bed	We must put everything away safe
7	Football (13 years)	Mimed game	We daren't lose again.

There appear to be three main features to the attitudes listed in the third column: (1) it is an attitude that the participants can draw upon from their past experience in *other contexts*; (2) it provides at least a temporary theme and a reality that a group can share a belief in, for example, for the six-year-olds the incipiently imagined monster threat started as 'putting things away safely' *because* of the monster; and (3) there is an implicit pressure or tension: life *must* go on; we *must* talk about ordinary things; we *daren't* lose again.

In addition to these obvious criteria, there are other significant implications in the list of examples. For instance you can probably guess that most of the actions are teacher-imposed, in that they are not PLOT actions (the exception might be 'Arriving at a planning meeting'). It is natural for children, in setting up the play for themselves to launch into action of plot. Northern Ireland means one group raiding another; robbing a bank means a police chase; monster means hunting with spears or guns in the forests. So here is the teacher using the selection of action and the attitude to go with it as a brake on the plot; not in their wildest dreams could chasing a monster start with 'going to bed'! So 'the play for the teacher' at this starting point takes priority over the children's play (nine times out of ten in my own experience, but the exceptions are always interesting). One point to mention here is that the topics were mostly the group's own democratic choice (this will be discussed later) so, to that extent, the initial thinking represents *their* play, although the first action represents the teacher's thinking. Even in the instance of 'Arriving at a planning meeting' although this particular action implies the start of a plot for a topic that is called 'Robbing a bank' it is clearly teacher's idea of plot, and the attitude 'Must not draw attention to ourselves' will still operate as a brake.

Why is it important to have such a brake? There are several related reasons. It gives the children chance to find a reality, an appropriateness of felt value that begins to seem right to them as participants and is objectively valid in terms of the context. 'Must fight boredom' may be an attitude that will allow the fourteen-year-olds time to find a reality in a situation that is right out of their experience – apart from television, and of course what they tend to remember from

61

television films and plays is the highlights of *plot*. So before they themselves rush into plot an exercise form of this kind brings an integrity to their experience. In other words a subsequent 'play for them' about, say, escaping from prison camp will now be coloured, at least, by this initial experience of fighting boredom.

Summary of first part of chapter

This has been a complex chapter so far, attempting as it does to introduce new models and terminology. I think a summary might be useful before I discuss further forms of exercise structure.

Type D, Drama for understanding, can be seen as being a combination of two sets of goals, the children's and the teacher's. I have suggested that, additionally, the 'play for the children' and the 'play for the teacher' represent two contrasting structures. The children's has the quality of Type B, Dramatic playing; the teacher's is either an exercise or theatre form. This chapter is confined to looking at exercise.

In examining both children's play and dramatic playing I have distinguished two functions, an instrumental function, 'I am making it happen', and a passive existential function, 'it is happening to me', and claimed that the exercise form in the 'play for the teacher' takes over or extends the instrumental function; he does not participate in the 'living-through' experience.

The instrumental function involves a process of particularisation. In play, when the child is his own agent, the process is seen as an affective impetus finding expression in a selected topic and a selected action within the topic. The action carries a value of significance to the child. In drama a similar process of particularisation takes place. When the teacher is the agent, he helps with the selection of a topic, the selection of an action and, most important, the selection of a value that can have both collective and personal significance. When he suggests to his class that the spies drank their beer without the pub's clientèle even noticing they were there, the teacher has selected an action and a meaning to the action that allows the drama to start with a sense of significance. The structure employed is virtually one of exercise. It is, however, 'folded in' in a way that releases the children into experiencing. Type D drama then is more than Type A, Exercise; it is more than Type B: Dramatic playing. It is an integration of the structures of both.

The kind of exercise form we have looked at however, has been limited to the very short-term particularisation process, an initiation into action. Other forms are referred to in the African list on p. 52. There are, however, three major, longer-term drama activities that structurally are close to exercise. They are: problem-solving drama; mantle of the expert; and contextual role-playing.

Before discussing these I make a temporary diversion in order to deal with a topic which has kept rearing its head in all the chapters and has relevance for our discussion of the above three structures: characterisation.

Characterisation – a misnomer

In all our discussions so far there has been no mention of that popular drama term, characterisation.

Looking at the list on p. 60 the only 'characters' stated either implicitly or explicitly appear to be 'we'. Now there are enormously important, subtle and sometimes paradoxical implications here. By immediately talking about 'we' – 'We must fight the boredom as we play this ball game yet again' rather than 'You will need to act at being bored when you *take the part of the prisoners*' – the teacher is assuming that the participants *are* the prisoners. But here is the paradox. It is not that in a Stanislavskian way they are playing their parts so well that they have *become* the prisoners. When the teacher assumes they 'are' he is not judging some impressively successful artistry. It is that the participants are themselves sharing an agreed attitude: 'life must go on'; 'talking about ordinary things in order to hide our thoughts';

'we want to please someone else'; 'we are failing and must not fail any more', etc. The reality of the situation lies in the value that is given to the context, not the context itself. So the conventional theatre-minded teacher is working from a totally different perspective when he sets as a goal the notion of 'becoming a character'. His vocabulary will be of 'portrayal', 'studying a part', 'casting according to type or against type', 'playing a role well or not well'. The Type D drama teacher will be interested in what steps a child takes to modify his own behaviour only in so far as the value identified is appropriate to the situation.

Another notion of 'becoming' can be found among those teachers who see drama as a cathartic experience where it is judged some children need to 'escape from themselves' for a while, so that 'becoming someone else' is a valuable therapy. A Type D drama teacher, as I pointed out at the end of Chapter 5, does not want children or adults to escape from who they are – rather the opposite. He wants a quality of hyper-awareness that is generated by this very ambivalence of being oneself but adopting an attitude, not necessarily one's own, relevant to some imagined context. It is this process of seeing oneself from a different angle that is the principal purpose of drama in education.

It is possible that in some kinds of good work in drama the gradual building up of a range of complex attitudes belonging to a particular role becomes equivalent to the conventional concept 'characterisation'. For instance, I have worked with a group of adults who over many sessions added more and more facets to their relationships *en famille* and in so doing could, in traditional theatre terms, have been described as 'creating well-rounded characters'. But this is not particularly relevant, for each stage of work was really a re-examination of themselves, as a new tension or pressure was applied. Even in script work I do not want a child to 'create' Shakespeare's Macbeth, but to look at himself as he identifies with some of the values implicit in the text.

Diversion over! And yet our discussion has been timely for it is interesting to look at the following exercise structures in terms of the demands they make (or do not make) on characterisation. In the following section I give many examples, in the hope that these will not only amply support this discussion on structure, but also supply the reader with ideas for his own work.

Problem-Solving Drama

Sometimes it is possible to start the drama by contriving a problem which is sufficiently interesting or curiosity-arousing in itself that activity can be started without the participants having to *identify* a relevant attitude, because, *extrinsically*, they are already motivated by the problem. When I said to a class of five-year-olds on one occasion (shaking and turning upside down a pottery vase as I did so), 'I don't know what to do; I've lost Tom Thumb; I put him safely in this vase last night and he's gone. What can I do?', the problem moved imperceptibly into the action of trying to find him. (He was eventually found at the top of a very tall tree, and 'How do you get him down when he refuses to come?' was the next problem.) Now in this kind of drama situation there is no group concern that impels them, before the drama started, towards a story; there was no question of establishing who 'they' were to be and what feeling qualities would be appropriate for 'them' to have in a 'searching for Tom Thumb' situation. The problem and the possibility of its resolution were enough to motivate the children to enter the make-believe. It is possible to use this method with people of all ages.

Examples
1 With a class of boisterous nine-year-olds who wanted a Haunted House theme I established that the house was heavily barred with only one (heavy iron) door, that they were not carrying oxyacetylene equipment or mechanical diggers for excavating tunnels under the house, that the only occupant was an ageing retainer (me) who would not open the door (which had four locks on it). He could be spoken to through a grating, but would not listen if his

suspicions were aroused in any way. These children worked hard for over half an hour trying some ingenious methods and eventually persuaded the retainer to open the door and let them in. (Note. Nine-year-olds had solved a problem: it was never established who 'they' were.)

2 With a class of educationally sub-normal twelve/thirteen-year-old boys who, in planning 'an escape from prison' were countered at every stage by a teacher who built in more and more devices to block their way. What I was doing, of course, was forcing them to refine their thinking so that they finally 'triumphed' with what was (for them) a very subtle plan. (Note. Again it was not established who 'they' were.)

3 A class of fourteen-year-olds chose a murder story. I asked them to agree that I could choose the murderer from among them without the rest knowing. This 'secret' between teacher and one student provided extrinsic impetus to get the dramatic activity started.

4 With a group of adults: 'The little girl in the other room was a witness to the armed robbery but unfortunately she is mentally subnormal and terrified of strangers. Work out and practise on each other how you propose to get the true facts from her.'

5 An example from Dorothy Heathcote, with a group of six-year-olds to whom it was explained that work had to be done in the kitchens, that there were available a number of robots (adult students) who could do it but they had to be programmed. Could the children manage to describe very carefully to the robots exactly what they would have to do? (The objective for the lesson incidentally was to get the children to use complete sentences.)

Each of the above is obviously more time-consuming than the exercises in the original list on p. 3. The motivation of solving a problem without even worrying about 'who they are supposed to be' can give an impetus that can last for more than one session, and, more important, the process of solving has its own built-in learning area.

The mantle of the expert

Linked with this problem form where a group of people actually solve a problem without necessarily knowing who they are supposed to be is another significant form: 'the mantle of the expert', where it is very important that the participants know who they are, but in a special way. This form was introduced to me by Dorothy Heathcote who regards it as not only having considerable educational potential but as the easiest dramatic form for the inexpert teacher to handle.

In 'the mantle of the expert' the children are endowed with a role from the beginning of the experience, the role of an expert – craftsman, designer, archaeologist, etc. – with an expertise that the teacher, usually in a different role, requires. Examples follow:

1 Teacher as emissary from King William I has called together world renowned architects (the class) to develop new designs for impregnable castles. (9-year-old pupils; lasted for two lessons.)

2 Teacher representing a West African government has invited world experts in all the Olympic games to advise his government on both training methods and training facilities. (13-year-old pupils who had asked to have some drama about sport; five lessons.)

3 An example by a Sunderland teacher: Teacher as government official offering money to experts in escapology to design an escape-proof prison for the world's most dangerous criminals. (12/13-year-old boys who had asked to do drama about 'escaping from prison'; five lessons.)

4 An example by a Gateshead teacher: Teacher as stranger who needs help from village family craftsmen – wheelwrights, farriers, apothecaries, farmers, etc. (6/7-year-old pupils; lasted *two terms*. This developed into a huge project. A more detailed account of how it started can be read in the Schools Council project, *Drama in Primary Schools* by Tom Stabler (1979).

5 An example from Dorothy Heathcote: Teacher as a landowner who needs to hire sheep-shearers. (10/11-

year-old pupils; one lesson.)

6 An example from Dorothy Heathcote: Children as monks, followers of the Venerable Bede, building the monastery at Jarrow. The activities included the *actual* making of bread, soup, and butter, in role throughout. (Two separate classes of 10/11 years and 6/7 years; lasted for five full consecutive sessions.)

7 An example from Dorothy Heathcote: Children as servants running a Tudor mansion. This was set in an actual Tudor mansion; the purpose of the exercise was to help pupils look at architectural style. (14-year-old pupils; two mornings.)

8 An example from Dorothy Heathcote: Children as factory workers in different departments (design; repairs; dispatch; personnel), making materials for invalids. (15/16-year-old pupils, bottom stream; each Friday afternoon for a whole year).

9 An example from Dorothy Heathcote: Designers of shirts in a shirt factory. (8/9-year-old pupils; one lesson.)

10 Examples from Dorothy Heathcote with adults: (*a*) as experts employed by the National Trust to 'restore' an eighteen-century manor house and (*b*) as designers of eighteenth-century gardens.

11 Teacher as representative of a Board of Education meeting selected staff of two senior high schools (American system) to plan the merger of the two philosophically contrasted schools. (15/16-year-old pupils; one lesson.)

Note. The reference to length of time in the above examples refers to drama timetabling. The follow-up time in many cases was considerable.

As in the problem form there is no initial seeking to identify an attitude belonging to the make-believe. There *is* an attitude required immediately, but it emanates from the actual situation: 'Here is teacher saying he doesn't know and that we do know.' In the example on Olympic games, the children, who five minutes earlier had shown great enthusiasm for the subject, were overwhelmed by a sense of being trapped into a commitment they were not sure they could carry through. This process of initially putting children at a disadvantage so that they can enjoy the self-esteem that comes as they realise (*a*) how much they do know (the 'ignorant' teacher has nothing but respect for every straw of knowledge that can be grasped), and (*b*) how rewarding it is to research what they do not know.

All the energies of the children in this kind of work resemble most normal curriculum activities: the class is reading, recording, discussing, planning, selecting, checking, evaluating; all the common educational skills are practised and a great deal of objective knowledge is obtained. Any skills to do with playing a role or creating a play are almost non-existent, unless, of course, teacher and class consciously turn the experience into something else. It is as though, having taken the initial step towards make-believe by accepting the mantle of expert sportsmen or sheep-shearers, etc., they can forget about it, just as we wear clothes and then for the most part forget about them.

There are two major kinds of growths possible in 'mantle of the expert'. One is an almost awesome understanding of a sense of responsibility. The other is a respect for expertise and for the objective world that has been studied. It seems to me that more than any other activity across the curriculum this particular form of drama can give children a glimpse of the meaning of scholarship.

Contextual role play

It makes a considerable contrast to swing now to what is a comparatively ordinary, 'functional' use of a dramatic exercise form. I have called it contextual role play, though it is an unsatisfactory use of terminology because for many people all role play is contextual. But I do not know what else to call this kind of exercise, which is usually recognised by the following features:

1 It usually gives the participants *practice* in some social skill.
2 It concentrates on *external* behaviour.

3 It often needs just a short span of time, from half a minute upwards.

4 The *purpose* is always clear to the participants.

5 The structure must be precise or the wrong thing will be practised!

6 There can be an immediate sense of achievement.

7 The finish of the exercise is usually clear.

The reader will see the kind of drama I mean from the following illustrations. The first five are taken from my work with psychiatric adult patients.

1 Some severely institutionalised women patients (they may have had twenty to thirty years in the hospital) were on a retraining scheme for going out to live once more in the community. For them the kind of exercise might be:

   (*a*) Simply answering the door, not knowing what register of behavioural response is required: it could be the rent man, the vicar, a kindly neighbour, an officious neighbour, a child who needs help, a salesman or a 'stranger' who wants to come in. The ability to recognise, understand and handle each of these in the best possible way is not something that can come easily to these patients who have only had to relate to a few 'kinds' of people during their stay in the institution.

   (*b*) Shopping practice: selecting presents for people.

   (*c*) Assessing other people's behaviour: recognising trustworthiness in other people; recognising other people's needs and points of view.

   (*d*) Tricky situations: how do you cope in the best possible way with the milkman who, in his hurry (he is running late) inadvertently has charged you too much?

2 Many short-term or middle-term neurotic patients lack the ability to assert themselves. One of the reasons for their being in the hospital (or for dreading leaving it) is that other people trample over them. Practice exercises might be:

   (*a*) Not allowing yourself to be manipulated by a friend over everyday items like how to spend the evening or what to buy for the house or what 'bargains' to be tempted by or 'just have one for the road' persuasion.

(b) Where assertion is required to stop someone else doing something stupid. (I should perhaps make it clear that I or another patient under my instruction role-plays 'the other' in all these scenes: the person at the door, the shopkeeper, the friend, etc. In each case one judges just how much pressure the patient can take. In this particular exercise, as the patient gains in assertion 'the other' presses even harder for even greater firmness; if there appears to be a lessening of confidence he takes off the pressure.)

(c) Applying for a job.

(d) Coping with being teased about having been in hospital.

3 Some patients simply need practice in socialising: (a) chatting with strangers in a pub; (b) talking to the opposite sex, etc.

4 Some need practice in coping with their own family's temperaments and idiosyncrasies.

5 Psychodramatic role-play: some patients are helped by using fellow patients to re-enact past painful experiences. (as in the 'attempted suicide' example described on p. 107.)

6 Role play can be used effectively with professional people whose work requires them to handle others with competence and trust. This vocational practice has been tried from time to time with social workers, probation officers, doctors, nurses, police, personnel officers and teachers.

7 Another use of role play for professionals gives practice in decision-making. Often a fairly complex simulation of a normal interaction is set up so that a group of participants can examine how they themselves arrive at decisions.

It is clear that the purpose of the above kinds of role-play exercises relate to the participants' own lives, often dealing with some social problem. In most cases they are required overtly to be 'playing themselves', as opposed to children really playing themselves under the guise of being pirates or, as in the problem exercises listed earlier in the chapter, where it is not established with any precision what the roles are.

Does this contextual role play have any place in our schools (all the examples I have given are from its use with hospital patients or vocational groups)? Already other subject areas, particularly geography, have supported the commercialisation of simulation games. Moral educationists seem to recommend this form of role play fairly strongly, often adopting a 'What would you do if . . . ?' structure where children are required to identify with various moral dilemmas close to their own lives; for example, 'What would you do if you discovered your friend had broken a promise to keep a secret you had shared with her?'

It seems to me that this kind of role play usefully provides a reference point, a visual aid, for class discussion. It varies in structure from a dramatic-playing mode of a simulation game where the decision-making is actually experienced, to the (more typically) simple demonstrating quality of a pure exercise where there is no question of 'living-through'. Apart from the simulation game, contextual role play is brief and episodic, often not the central activity of a lesson. It has value for many teachers across the curriculum but, paradoxically, as drama it perhaps has least educational potential.

Questions

1 Give examples from your own drama teaching experience of 'play for the children' combined with 'play for the teacher'. Do you consider this is a useful model?
2 How does the author appear to have changed from Chapter 1 in the way he is now discussing the concept of 'exercise'?

7 Dramatic structure – theatre

The last chapter moved us nearer to understanding Type D drama. Whereas in the opening chapter 1 classified two of the drama forms as Type A, Exercise and Type B, Dramatic playing, I have now tried to establish that in any creative drama activity there can be two plays going on at the same time, the play for the participants in a dramatic-playing mode and the play for the teacher in a more structured mode. In the last chapter the structure we examined was exercise. The levels of meaning that seem to emerge from this structure were: (*a*) single identification with an attitude that is appropriate to the role and has more universal application; (*b*) problem-solving, where there is virtually no identification with a role; (*c*) mantle of the expert, where there is specific identification but only in respect of expertise and responsibility; and (*d*) contextual role play, where some aspect of social interaction is practised.

None of these structures, alone, would stand up as an art form. A student of mine recently suggested to me that placing the emphasis on drama for *learning* in fact does a disservice to the art form. I can understand how he reached that conclusion although in fact the opposite is true. If we take yet another look at the 'African' lesson we could detect elements that are unmistakeably theatrical in form. In Chapter 6 I tried to establish that in Type D drama there is a necessary blending of dramatic playing and exercise. I now want to make the point that theatre form can also be 'folded in'. This will be discussed in some detail later, but for now let me say that just as it was stressed in Chapter 4 that psychological progress towards the art form was dependent on collective, cognitive and affective sharing of a focus of attention, the cohesive, elevating force that makes that focus possible is a theatre form. It is often not enough for children to be 'busy trapping a lion' (dramatic playing) nor for teacher to say 'Let's work out how deep the trap should be' (exercise), for if the experience does not take on qualities that have the tension, the density, the immediacy of action coupled with the non-immediacy of meaning that belong to theatre, there is less chance of collective sharing taking place. The drum-beat signalling the news from one end of the classroom to the other must transcend the original exercise ('What are the different messages that can be conveyed by drum-beat to the old man left behind?'); and it must in a moment of riveted attention convey all that the group knows, and more, about the sending and receiving of good and bad news.

Similarly, the ritualisation of meal-taking, passing the communal bowl of fou-fou round the circle; the ceremony of placing living flowers in the earth in front of each hut as a symbol that home is a leaving and a returning; the rhythmic snake-like tribal line of tramping feet round the classroom to represent the length of the journey and the passing of time; the tension created by the 'old man' asking to be left behind just when we were at the very edge of a big adventure; the silent, immobile waiting in the dark for the lion; the whispered messages from their leader 'high up in a tree'; the arm movements in unison as we paddled the raft back to our own shores: all these actions elevate the dramatic playing and the functionary exercise to a level of symbolisation that places the work firmly in an artistic form and makes modification of meaning more accessible.

And this is where I complete the paradox. As already mentioned in Chapter 3, we do not want the children to be mesmerised by the experience but to be finely *aware* of what is happening to them and of their responsibility in it. So in fact they *are*, in part, watching themselves from the outside, not because they want to be effective for the sake of someone else but because the opportunity for heightened understanding is intuitively recognised. This quality of consciousness of self is very different from the self-conscious hybrid acting form mentioned earlier.

The richness of the 'African' experience for the Californian six-year-olds lay in the power of the symbolic use of action and object – the power of theatre, in fact. This chapter attempts to define some of the elements that appear to raise the level of the work to a significance of form that could be described as art. The ways in which this more significant form affects 'negotiation of meaning', a term so usefully coined by the Schools Council (Secondary) Drama Project, will also be discussed. But first let me make it quite clear that it is dramatic *structure* with which we are concerned. The existential mode is not taken away; indeed it can be enhanced by the introduction of structures that a playwright would happily employ in his writing.

In the Schools Council Drama (Secondary) Project publication, *Learning through Drama*, in their understandable anxiety not to appear to give too much emphasis to differences between drama and theatre, the authors (McGregor *et al*, 1977) fail to make this point, that whereas in terms of structure there is rich common ground for the participant, the psychological demands are significantly different. It is the common ground that I shall attempt to analyse in this chapter: common ground because in a conventional theatre it operates for an audience, heightening their experience; in Type D drama it operates for the participants, heightening *their* experience. The distant, initially indistinct sounds that might be Grendel's lumbering step breaking the silence are as awesome for Beowolf's nine-year-old 'warriors' as for a nine-year-old audience – both experience the simultaneous wanting to hold back and inviting the inevitable.

Theatre form

I recall being told in the first lecture I ever attended on theatre studies that the principal elements were CONFLICT, CONTRAST and SURPRISE. I propose to use this classification here, but with some modification. I prefer to use the word TENSION rather than conflict, to subsume surprise under tension and to add SYMBOLISATION as a category. In some ways it is obvious that they are not separate headings at all, that contrast and symbolisation are all part of tension. Indeed it will be difficult at times to discuss any one without reference to the others. Nevertheless, even if it is just for the practical reason that this is going to be a long chapter filled with anecdotal illustration, such a classification will help the reader to find his way around.

A. Tension

1   A sense of time

The use of the word CONFLICT (discussed further in Appendix 1) has misled many teachers into assuming that drama cannot start unless there is some dramatic clash of views, beliefs, opinions or temperaments. I have watched many groups of children or even adults trained in theatre enter improvised drama on this assumption – I used to do it myself! All over the drama world one can find enemies who have battles, friends who quarrel, councillors who hold opposing views and husbands and wives who wrangle. Dramatic tension is a more subtle, more powerful quality of enemies who search for ways to delay the battle, of friends who might choose to be dishonest rather than quarrel, of councillors who bury their differences because of a new outside threat (the Pied Piper again!), of husbands and wives who share a burden, not disagree about it. The tension is there because the conflict might be round the corner. It is this looking to the future because of what we do now, coupled with the knowledge that what we do now belongs to what we and others did in the past, that characterises the drama experience. Susanne Langer (1953) puts it: 'Theatre ... moves not towards the present as narrative does but towards something beyond; it deals eventually with commitments and consequences.' She goes on, 'It has been said repeatedly that theatre creates a perpetual moment; but it is only a present filled with its own future that is really dramatic.' It is this sense of time that does not rest in the present but is continually looking backwards and forwards that carries a *tension* of commitments and consequences. For further elaboration on this and other points in this chapter see my article, 'Creative drama as an art form', [Bolton, 1977]).

2 Focus

The 'sense of time' tension is related to the attitude of mind of the participants rather than to theatrical structure. Focus on the other hand is what the playwright selects in terms of specific action and/or place. Shakespeare has Prince Henry wander in disguise among his men before Agincourt; Romeo gatecrashes a ball; the ghost of Banquo attends a feast. The tensions in these scenes send off ripples of meaning that reflect many of the themes that the plays are about. So, too, in drama this kind of structuring must be made available to the participants. If the children do not supply it themselves then the teacher must adopt this function of a playwright. Here are some examples from past lessons.

(*a*) The Newcastle advisory teacher team were required to work with ten and eleven-year-olds on the Jacobite Rebellion. Their chosen focus was the capturing by the Scottish soldiers of an English soldier who claimed to like the Scots. All the potential for exploring what the war was about is inherent within that context.

(*b*) A similar age group I was working with chose Florence Nightingale for their drama. 'The play for them' was to do with nursing (girls) and having injuries (boys). I had selected the learning area of 'concept of authority' as the Scutari hospital situation was fraught with problems of who was to make decisions and where Florence Nightingale's authority stood in relation to the women she had brought over from England compared with where it stood in relation to the doctors who wanted her and her women shipped back to England. The focus of a locked cupboard containing extra blankets, its key held securely by Dr Hall, provided a vehicle for the tension between the women who wanted to nurse in their way and the doctors (the boys of the class were split into patients and doctors) who would not let them.

(*c*) A class of six-year-olds wanted to do a play about Snow White having an adventure with the Three Bears. The focus became our returning (we were dwarfs of course) to our house at the end of a working day, anticipating but not getting the usual welcome. The search, the finding of a note left by Snow White, mysteriously interrupted in its writing, all allowed the dangers the story might be about to be felt. Again the focus established an appropriate tension.

(*d*) A group of five-year-olds who wanted 'hunting a strange creature'. The focus I chose was bringing in my 'baby' (a folded up cardigan) that had a very unusual scratch on its face. The advantage of this kind of focus is that the initial action is to do with attending to a scratch in a way that *carries the implications* to do with the larger problem of hunting the creature.

(*e*) Likewise for a group of eight- to twelve-year-olds who wanted, as 'mad scientists', to destroy the world by building a robot, the focus became (*a*) problems of building the robot, and (*b*) problems of controlling it. The experience of destroying was therefore savoured in the disciplined co-operation of making and controlling; the actions of wiring the electric circuits, etc. were done in anticipation of the destruction.

(*f*) A group of thirteen- to fourteen-year-olds who chose a play about a haunted house. The focus was me in role in a pub demanding money from them if I was to risk guiding them to '*that place*'. If they had heard what I'd heard . . . but then, it wasn't for me to open me mouth . . .

3 Surprise

Just as an audience can be led by the nose to anticipate the wrong outcome or be kept in the dark, so the participants in creative drama can enjoy this experience. An obvious example is one I mentioned earlier where a group of adolescents did not know who the 'murderer' was, but a teacher can use more subtle devices:

(*a*) In the drama described earlier about camping, where the second dimension was 'we must put up out tents with efficiency in order to please the scoutmaster', these particular children enjoyed and were skilled in miming so it was with some pride that they carried out the task. Imagine their astonishment when I as their new scout-master remained unimpressed and, indeed, critical. Their disappointment turned to anger when it became apparent that I had no sense of fairness in my subsequent dealings. So as the play proceeded they plotted their revenge, choosing my departure 'to go to the village' as an opportunity to wreck my tent. I returned to give them a second surprise. I had been ill-tempered up to now – but, having been for a drink in the local, I was now benign. The tension became unbearable when, instead of stumping into my tent as usual, I stayed with them and tried to chat amicably over 'cocoa'. Then, when at last, I bid them a cheerful 'goodnight' their third surprise came with my reaction – they had expected a burst of fury and had mentally prepared themselves to cope with invective and punishment. What they got, however, was a scoutmaster who 'went all silent and hurt'.

(*b*) One of the 'mantle of the expert' exercises outlined in the last chapter was that of a class of thirteen- and fourteen-year-old boys building an escape-proof prison. For the first three lessons (once a week, forty minutes each) the mode had been simply to demonstrate their expertise in planning and building and testing. For the fourth lesson the class teacher and I planned to change the dramatic quality of the experience. I role-played a visitor repre-senting some unnamed European government that, impressed by the possibility of an escape-proof prison, had sent me to investigate what were the realistic pos-sibilities of building such a place in my country. With enthusiasm the experts stood up to my scepticism answering my most challenging questions and demon-strating how everything was computer-controlled from a nerve centre of the prison. As planned, the class teacher and I in our roles suddenly 'turned the tables' and using our newly acquired knowledge, took over the prison, with the experts as prisoners. We explained that this very expertise made them very powerful, dangerous men who could be corrupted into misusing their unique knowledge; that in fact that prison and others like it, could only be escape-proof when their knowledge was not available to the world. . . . A different *kind* of drama had now begun.

(c) An example of finding a 'starting' attitude in the last chapters was that of a class of thirteen-year-olds in a Sunderland school who wanted to do a play about Northern Ireland, in which we started the action in a supermarket with the attitude that 'life must go on'. Although I offered that list of exercises on page 60 as examples of 'making a start' by finding some attitude that would be both true for the context (in this case Northern Ireland with children who had never been there but who knew about the violence from newspapers and television) and would have a universal meaning that the pupils could tap – 'life must go on' is what the play could, initially at any rate, be about. It is rare, however, that a teacher's thinking fails to go beyond getting it started. He is not likely, in an arbitrary way, to think: 'Northern Ireland. Ah yes! "life must go on" – Ah yes! supermarket.' For he could have thought of 'Taking extra care to lock your doors at night', or 'How do you watch a stranger in a pub without him knowing you are watching?', or 'When there is a pile of bricks in a street and someone says "throw" how hard is it not to?' Any of these and many more would have been true to the context.

The early selection therefore is based on several clues – for instance the restlessness level of the class might suggest the throwing stones start rather than the locking up the house to go to sleep start. But in this particular case I had been given a clue from the discussion that took place before the drama started. The boys of this mixed class had been eager to divide themselves into IRA and Provos. The girls had said they were not going to take sides – they were 'going to keep their noses clean'. As teacher I now knew what I hoped the children might begin to understand: that if you are there you cannot fail to be drawn in.

So the starting attitude I encouraged them to select was ironical – it fitted the position they were taking but it also provided the appropriate tension for what the final outcome was going to be (it is like pulling a bow backwards so that the arrow can fly forwards). The innocence of shopping gradually became a background against which a violent incident between the IRA and the Provos (arranged and carried out by the boys) took place. The IRA and the Provos disappeared; the only ones left were the women in the shop in front of whose large glass windows it had all happened. The 'women' were whisked off for questioning by a 'brutal' police officer (teacher in role) who was not prepared to accept the women's word that they had not seen the incident clearly enough because it was all over in a flash. The girls, under this kind of pressure, were resentful, angry, upset and astonished.

Something of the misery and hopelessness of the Irish situation dawned on them that lesson. Two Belfast teachers happened to be watching. They commented afterwards that it had been 'real' for them too.

(*d*) The above use of surprise is effective only if the shock tactics centre on and open up the conceptual target the teacher has in mind. Sometimes another kind of objective can be the target. In the 'African' series of lessons with young children discussed in Chapter 5, I, who in role as a member of the tribe had been somewhat directorial in helping them to prepare for the journey and in the 'lion capture practice', suddenly announced that because of my great age the journey was becoming too much for me and would they please just leave me behind and pick me up again on the way back. I felt these particular seven-year-olds needed the experience of independence and group responsibility.

(*e*) On another quite different occasion a group of very bright sixteen- to eighteen-year-olds had chosen to start a new society by emigrating to a different planet. Throughout the work they were very articulate about which values, social, economic, political and scientific,

81

they wished to preserve from life on Earth but every time the question of *spiritual* values cropped up they avoided the issue and hurriedly switched back to, for example, planning accommodation for communal living. So, in the last of the five sessions, I died! I had been a respected member of their community: they could not ignore my body. Whatever they did with it, had to reflect where they wanted to stand in terms of belief about life and death.

Before moving on to the next kind of theatrical device, contrast, let me remind the reader that 'surprise' can only be employed where 'the play for them' is in a dramatic playing, existential mode. If the children themselves were in a theatre mode they could not experience the surprise but could only work out technically how to make surprise an experience for the audience.

B. Contrast

There are times in the work when the use of surprise is just not relevant: the warriors *know* that Grendel is going to come and even if it is supposed to be that moment of the story related to Grendel's first visit the children who already know the story cannot *genuinely* be surprised. So if the feeling quality cannot be surprise, then some other quality will be needed to give the experience integrity. It is the *way* in which Grendel arrives that is important and if some initially indeterminate sounds are followed by unmistakably heavy, advancing steps, it is this use of sound against a contrasting background of silence that turns an anticipated experience into an awesome one.

Similarly using a single movement against a background of stillness brings a quality to the moment in *Treasure Island* when a ship hand leaves the group of watching mates and approaches Long John Silver with the black spot proffered. That the child playing Long John is standing some distance away, a man alone looking across at a huddle of waiting men, is all part of the stock-in-trade of the 'theatre' director;

whereas a director would have blocked that contrast in grouping, the teacher either imperceptibly contrives it or harnesses it when it happens accidentally so that the children *sense* the implied meaning in that particular use of space and grouping. Put a child on a high dais as a king and you are doing three things, two of which are important for this kind of work: (1) you are helping the child by use of this physical pointer to 'feel' status; (2) you are helping other participants to perceive and believe in that child's status; and (3) *if* there were an audience it would also say status to them – but that is an irrelevance; indeed (3) is often not catered for at all. If a teacher were to put children under a table covered with a cloth right down to the floor so that they experience something of close proximity, claustrophobia and a limited visual field in a drama about being trapped, none of these experiences would be available to any one who happened to be watching. Indeed an uninformed or unimaginative head-teacher passing through might have his own interpretation of what was going on!

Another important kind of contrast we have met in previous illustrations: the contrast of *directions*. When the campers were carrying out revenge their scoutmaster was mellowing; when the women in the Irish supermarket were secure in normality, that was the moment of threat; when the prison experts were at their most confident, the tables were turned.

C. Symbolisation

In some ways this section might be considered to be the most important part of this book, for it is this particular facet of theatre that is related to *depth* of meaning in drama in education. If I may quote from that very fine account of Dorothy Heathcote's philosophy written by Betty Jane Wagner (1976, p. 76) 'True gut-level drama has to do with what you at your deepest level want to know about what it is to be human.'

I mentioned earlier that a student of mine had suggested

that by placing the emphasis on learning objectives a teacher might be doing a disservice to the art form. It is perhaps in this sense of knowing at the deepest level that the student may justifiably have detected some neglect from teachers, myself among them, who attempt to be precise in what they are teaching. 'Knowing at the deepest level' suggests something that cannot be articulated and is therefore not accessible to the terminology of educational objectives; this is especially true where objectives have to be spelled out in behavioural terms.

When Bruner (1974), watching a girl, Cathy, who had been shocked at seeing a film of a seagull stoned to death and had cried out in class, 'He's not even human doing that to a seagull,' commented, 'She was hard at work in her rage on the conjecture what makes human beings human' (p. 81), his very phrasing implies, as does B.J. Wagner's, a dialectic between the subjective and objective that cannot be finally resolved into objective knowledge. Cathy's final understanding will be more than a list of criteria which objectively distinguish man from animals; it will include a 'sensing' about man's 'humanness' that defies articulation in conventional discursive form.

Mary Warnock (1976), in summarising Kant's view of imagination, says that "what we appreciate or create in the highest art, is a symbol of something which is forever beyond it." (P. 63) The implication here is that whatever meaning a symbol may ordinarily denote, whatever that 'something' is, in art further elusive meanings accrue. In fact we do not have to be in art to find ripples of meaning beyond that denoted immediately by a word, an action or a conception. We may use a word as a metaphor: 'tight-fisted' can have both a literal and implied meaning; putting a ring on a third finger of the left hand carries both actual and representational meanings; a boy's conception of his bedroom may go beyond the functional – it may stand for privacy or refuge or personal identity rather than just a place to sleep in.

I shall now argue that it is one of the principal functions of a teacher in Type D drama to help the participants work towards meanings beyond the literal. But the curious paradox

84

is that drama relies upon the most concrete form of experiencing – ACTION. Its power lies in concreteness, but its potential for meaning lies in symbolisation. In the past much emphasis has been placed on training children in their drama to imitate the actions of life with some accuracy – you can find many books that advise the teacher on 'threading-the-needle', 'digging-the-garden', 'miming carrying things', etc. The major principle behind the use of this kind of skill-training in fact orientates the pupils *away* from an art form, because it singles out merely the functional meaning of the actions. Deeper learning can only be made available when the meaning is released from the concrete. (I discuss this point further in an article in *Young Drama*, [Bolton, 1978a].)

Let us look at some examples. Take an instance from Dorothy Heathcote's teaching when towards the end of a few hours' work with a group of adolescents, she asked a youth to get a mop and bucket so that he could mop the floor as part of the play they were creating. The action could not have been more concrete. Using water from the bucket he diligently washed the floor of the hall they were working in. So what could be remarkable about that? you may be asking.

The fictitious setting was a prison. It was to be a criminal's last morning before going to the electric chair. There is still nothing remarkable about the use of a bucket in this context – until you take into account who these adolescents were. This was an 'approved school' as it used to be called, where young offenders were compulsorily housed because of their anti-social behaviour. In the drama Dorothy Heathcote was creating a prison for young people who were already prisoners; as their 'drama' scene began each inmate was lying with eyes closed on his bed listening to the early morning sounds. More than anything else, for these particular boys, the swish of a mop on the floor symbolised captivity and servility (washing the floors was a daily routine). That single action and sound made that morning in prison unbearably real for all of them, for the condemned man and his mates.

The effectiveness of a symbol therefore, whether it be action or object or both, is dependent on its concreteness and on its power to stir deep feelings in the people concerned. To a group of socially secure, middle-class, conforming adolescents doing a play about prison the use of a bucket might have been neutral or even amusing. Some other symbol would have to be found for them – the barber's scissors perhaps or emptying the slops or having their letters censored. But supposing it is a class of six-year-olds enjoying being captured by the wicked Giant, what would symbolise captivity (and size) for *them*? Taking their shoes off them and hanging them out of reach might be near the mark, or having a huge key at the giant's belt.

The choice of symbol is obviously crucial: it must be something that can hold as many levels of meaning as possible simultaneously. A few years ago I was working with John Fines and Ray Verrier in a junior school. The topic for the ten- to eleven-year-olds was the Dust Bowl of America when, in the 1930s, farmers in the mid-West were forced to leave their homes or starve. The obvious haven was the other side of the Rockies, the rich lands of California. They were not made welcome; they were either sent back or put in camps. In their drama the children experienced, in families, the packing up to leave home (the focus chosen for this was the ugly, desperate business of booking a truck-driver for the journey – you knew he would wring you dry, but you could not do much about it) and then, in a dramatic playing form they crossed the Rockies.

The elements of the next stage of the experience had to include arriving in a land of plenty; an abundance that they were not allowed to share; being rejected and humiliated. What would say both 'This is California' *and* 'Keep off'? As I mused on this in the school lunch-hour John Fines suggested, 'Why not try an orange?'

With their eyes closed they listened to my narration of the dawn: 'They had struggled through many trials; the physical hardships had been such many thought they would never make it but this morning their trucks were parked on gentler slopes and in the near distance the early sun shone on the green lushness of California. Open your eyes and make your descent.' What they met was a Californian (teacher in role)

86

standing on a rock (chair) to peer at them as they made their approach (across the space of the school hall). He had an orange in his hand. 'What you folks doing trespassing? Don't you know this is private property?' The class were ready to play the drama game with enthusiasm, but when the Californian started to eat his orange, dropping the peel at their feet, it suddenly wasn't a game: it was an insult. (What better illustration could you have of the necessary dialectic between the concrete and the abstract than this – the very smell of the orange meant both olfactory stimulation and injustice).

Their immediate reaction was the one to be expected from ten-year-olds who feel insulted, and they shouted their abuse. But their intelligence worked after a time; they withdrew and planned a new approach, an apologetic one. In fact they verbally grovelled to the Californian farmer, who listened to them (as he ate his second orange) and then said, 'I'm glad you Okies have had the decency to apologise. Now go back to where you came from.'

They were astonished and angry. I became teacher again and they told me in no uncertain terms what they felt about my inhumanity. John Fines stepped in at this point saying, 'And that was how it was.' He then filled them in with further historical data, for which, not surprisingly, they were avid. An interesting point to note here is that whereas at first the dramatic form controlled and indeed modified the expression of anger, at the end of the lesson their feelings were further contained and harnessed for the exploration of historical subject matter. In these terms therefore this illustration represents for me a classic instance of the practice of education. I wish we were able to train teachers to help children 'feel their way into knowledge'.

The choice of the symbol in the above example (eating an orange to represent ownership and territory rights) was selected with care and was immediately effective. But sometimes the use of an object or action starts in a manner that can only be described as perfunctory and appears to be an unlikely candidate for the task of symbolic representation. I recall vividly working with a group of adults who set up their drama in an Indian temple. They were supposed to be tourists. I say 'supposed' for the whole thing started very much tongue-in-cheek. Our sense of credibility was stretched to the uttermost when a pile of chairs, 'supposed' to be some temple statue, got accidentally knocked over. It was hastily rebuilt and stood there, a symbol of our embarrassment rather than anything else, looking singularly like what it was – a pile of chairs. This was a four-day course, and as we worked at our temple theme, that 'damaged statue' became more real for all of us until we reached a point where it variously symbolised our sense of being in a land where strange things could happen, to a sense of abnormal forces affecting our personal relationships. Indeed it became noticeable towards the end of the four days that even when we were not 'in the play' as it were, we tended to avoid walking near that pile of chairs – it could have been simply for practical safety reasons for some, but for others it had become a taboo area.

A more obvious use of symbols in drama is to use objects that are already evocative; an orange or a pile of chairs do not have this quality. A teacher or the children themselves search round for a sword, a cross, a diamond, a begging bowl, rosary beads, a uniform, a Bible, a skull, a flag. These are all objects that by themselves promote meaning. But there are other kinds of objects where the initial meaning might be but functional, where the teacher's mind must allow a freer movement to universals which might in turn be taken up by the children. So a box might in the teacher's mind imply wealth, travel, security or burden, and a key might mean possessions, safety, power, responsibility or escape. If the *teacher* cannot see beyond a box as a box or a key as a key he is likely to stay, and unwittingly encourage the children to stay, in the most superficial dramatic playing level.

Questions

1 Discuss the significance of what the author calls the symbolisation process. Draw on your own experience to

illustrate your discussion.
2 To what extent is a teacher adopting the function of playwright?
3 In what ways do the author's views of theatre appear to have changed from the first chapter?

8 Prerequisites for drama

I have spent seven chapters attempting to persuade the reader to see drama in education as a means of changing understanding and offering him a theoretical basis for analysing the different structures available to the teacher who pursues this particular goal. There has been the danger that in giving so much emphasis to the importance of affective/cognitive growth, I have unwittingly conveyed a sense of exclusiveness to some readers, a sort of 'change in values or nothing' view of drama. This chapter begins the process, carried on for the rest of the book, of broadening out the picture.

The argument has been that the central learning area in drama involves some kind of adjustment in the subjective meaning, a change in 'felt value' in respect of something in the objective world, or, rather, a change in respect of *me* in the objective world. Learning in drama represents a growth in personal knowledge as pointed out in the last chapter in the quotation from Bruner (p.84). Cathy's insight into man's 'humanness' was not simply that she was now equipped with new ways of categorising behaviour impersonally (although this is important) but that she now gave a new personal value to such knowledge.

This personal shift in value is for me the essential goal in drama teaching. The reader must now be asking (indeed the question may well have been at the back of his mind from the start), how *realistic* a goal is this? In practice how often is this shift in value actually achieved? And my answer has to be that, in my experience, *not very often*! Given the present stage of teacher-training in drama and a general lack of understanding of education for values, combined with such practical matters as timetable provision for the subject, many teachers stand little chance of ever reaching this kind of goal.

A depressing picture? Certainly, but there are at least two reasons why we should not allow ourselves to be defeated by it. One is that an equivalent question put to other subject specialisms might not receive any more encouraging answers. What would a mathematician reply to the challenge, 'How often do secondary maths teachers succeed in teaching new mathematical *principles* to average pupils as opposed to simply giving the pupils the key to solving further mathematical problems?'

But this use of unanswerable rhetoric as a defence is indulgent and unhelpful. There are fortunately more positive reasons for accepting that learning may not occur even when the teacher holds it as a principal goal and is trained in handling the relevant processes. There are some compensations on the way! The setting up of drama with a potential for affective/cognitive development appears to be dependent on certain prerequisites: elements which must be present for the drama to occur. Many of us from time to time find ourselves struggling in our teaching because one of these essential elements is eluding the work. In these instances finding it becomes a teacher's top priority, often *at the expense* of any other apparently more worthwhile goal he may have in mind. In this chapter I claim that when a prerequisite of drama becomes an immediate goal, the struggle and success in achieving it can often be assessed in educational terms as worthwhile.

That this can be so was brought home to me recently at the 1978 Riverside Conference, London, organised by Gerald Chapman, when at the end of three sessions of teaching a class of twelve-year-olds, I was feeling exhilarated from the experience, sensing that the children had left feeling six inches taller and that something worthwhile had been achieved. My self-indulgent satisfaction was brought abruptly to an end when one of the observers came up to me over lunch to tell me that I had failed and that I had taken up three very long sessions ($1\frac{1}{4}$ hours each) to do so; that although the children had gone out feeling pleased with themselves, they should not have done so because they had not really achieved anything. The startling thing was that this observer was using the very criteria that I myself invariabily use in assessing achievement. To what extent did the children finish up thinking more deeply or rationally or intelligently about the subject? 'They revealed the same type of shallow, stereotyped thinking with which they had started,' she challenged. And she was right.

And yet I knew, in my bones, that important things had happened. I propose to describe the three lessons in some detail so that we may examine elements which appear to be necessary phases in a process.

Place. Riverside Studios, London.

Environment. An old television studio turned into a theatre by placing a block of raked seats in the middle.

Occasion. Three lessons, Saturday morning, Saturday afternoon and Sunday morning, in front of an audience (a different audience each time) of people from education and from theatre. The audience of observers are confined to that block of seats, looking very much like an audience as we, the class and I, sit below them.

Class. Twelve-year-olds (lower band).

I have explained the location because we carried the burden of that location for most of the first two lessons. If ever a place was performance-oriented that was. So there were two crucial factors affecting the work before we even start:

1 Their expectations of what will be required of them, coming to a theatre on a Saturday morning; this in turn is affected by what their assumptions are about drama in the first place.

2 The kind of statement the place itself signals to them when they arrive.

Session One:

Choosing a theme

The class were faced with a paradox from the beginning. Their 'performance' assumptions were confirmed by the environment but here was a teacher signalling process, not product.

92

Action	*Comment*
1 I began by asking them what theme would be interesting to work at for three sessions, getting them to bring their chairs round the blackboard so that they had their backs to the audience.	Given the pressure on these children many teachers would have introduced some games at this point. This ploy has an obvious immediate advantage but my thinking tends to be that in a first lesson with a strange class where sharing with them my way of working (which I suppose, roughly, is that at every step we *think* our way into the next step) must have top priority, I do not want to introduce anything that misleads them on this. So in some ways I actually *increase* the tension, on the assumption that it pays dividends in the long run.
2 From a list of about six topics they voted fairly evenly between 'Classroom' and 'Violence' and then suggested combining them.	Notice that having been given the topic by the class, I do not now discuss how it should be set up. I have already warned them that I will make decisions. In other words *their* topic is going to start on *my* terms. Many readers might take issue with me here, but I keep fairly firmly to the following rules: (*a*) Where a class and I know each other fairly well the responsibility for how to start can lie much more heavily on their shoulders. (*b*) Some topics even where I do not know a class need probing further before it is possible to guess at what would be a productive start.

For instance, if they had chosen 'Victorian England' I would need to know much more about what aspect stirred their interest.

(*c*) For other topics (and 'Classroom and violence' is one of them) one can make fairly safe assumptions about what they mean and the focus of the initial dramatic action should *protect them into* the theme. There are two experiences that the teacher must not give them at this point: a chance for actual unstructured violence (of which there was no danger in this instance); and a scene requiring violent dramatic action which would fail out of sheer embarrassment – this applies especially strongly to these audience-oriented circumstances but tends in any case to be true for most classes choosing such topics. The most dramatic scenes (particularly group scenes) of real life tends to be the most undramatic and unreal in drama). So 'protecting them into their theme' is a golden rule for me.

3 By way of preparation for teacher role play I demonstrated the notion of picking up clues from teacher in role, using one or two children in sample scenes. The class were anxious and self-conscious but I gave it

This has its own dangers. Unless the balance is right, you may have simply invited them to be flippant for the rest of the work.

94

a light touch so that we could
'have a bit of a laugh', the
implication being that this
brief interlude is 'not for real'.

First focus in action – *Dramatic playing/theatre form*

4 I asked them to place their
chairs in a square facing
inwards. I suddenly became
a headmaster who had called a
staff meeting to discuss the
growth of violence in school,
referring mysteriously to the
'shocking' incident that had
happened yesterday. With a
few giggles they reported on
incidents of violence they had
as staff observed recently.

This allows them to bring out
into the open how they appear
to want to treat the subject;
the imagery of 'terrible
deeds in the classroom' can
hang in the air but it is
encapsulated in a form at
several removes from the
action itself. (A theatrical
device as old as the Greeks!)

    They tended to be quite
mild things like stealing or
breaking pencils or smashing
windows. I built up more
heavily the idea that all this
bad behaviour was capped by
'what happened yesterday'.
'Which form was it?' I asked.
'5D,' a child replied. I sensed
a rousing of interest in its
being a fifth form and I
therefore wanted to give them
a chance to be thoughtfully
selective in what they wanted
'violence from a fifth form'
to mean, so I, in role,
terminated the staff meeting,
leaving this 'very serious'
matter for discussion at a
special meeting.

We later christened that
class 5Q – I was afraid that
they might have particular
pupils in mind and that we
should safely distance it into
the fictitious.

Planning

5 I put them into small groups
to select the serious incident,

That some inattentiveness and
dissipating behaviour crept

having first discussed with the class what the differences might be between being twelve and sixteen years of age. Level of answers were quite thoughtful. In their small groups, however, motivation appeared to slacken.

in at this point took me by surprise as I assumed that the task of selecting a shocking school incident would generate interest. So what could be going wrong for them? The following are some of the possibilities:

(*a*) They were becoming 'turned-off' this teacher.
(*b*) They were being made to think too much.
(*c*) They were not being given the chance to perform to the audience.

It is worth noting here that during lunch-break three comments only were made to me by the children: 'When are we going to play games – we were told we'd play games' and 'Why can't we make up some little plays in our groups to show *them* (the audience)' and 'We don't have to carry on with the same thing this afternoon, do we? At school we always start with something new.'

(*d*) Their small group dynamics may tend to undermine their ability to work towards a 'discussion' task; the opposite of this proved to be the case in the second session, when they were allowed to 'rehearse'.
(*e*) The way this theme was now being handled was frustrating to them because they really wanted their

'violence kicks'; this point
cropped up immediately after
the session in discussion with
the observers, one of whom
felt very strongly that in
depriving them of their
'dining-room' experience the
outcome was less than
satisfactory. The implication
appeared to be that as a
teacher I was dodging what
was important to the children.
(I meet this point of view very
often.) This particular man
expressed himself forcibly, in
full certainty that he was
right. I was equally arrogant
in the knowledge of my golden
rule, that they needed
'protecting into' what they
had asked for. But this same
point was raised as an issue by
my lady critic who had
watched both the first and the
third session: 'If only,' she
said, 'you had allowed them
to have their violence in that
first session, the subsequent
work might have been more
thoughtful.' The point she is
making is important, but it
seems to me that she is failing
to recognise that certain
components must be present
before young people can gain
even limited satisfaction from
the very action they are asking
for. If their actual mood is one
that is constrained by the
circumstances (in this
instance, by exposure to an
audience; to a new teacher in

a new place; to a new way of working) then the only scenes they can begin with are those that allow them legitimately to operate with constraint (in this instance, being in a staff meeting) *only when they can trust this situation will they release the energy that a violently active scene requires.* But even though my judgement as teacher may be correct here, it does not necessarily alleviate their sense of frustration that they ought to be doing something different.

Back as a whole group to make selection, they chose a dining-room incident from among others such as 'being caught climbing through the window' and 'taking your trousers down in front of the girls in the classroom'.

Further whole group action – Dramatic playing/theatre form
(The slackening attention had tightened again).

7   We returned to the staff room, this time entering with some attempt at outward impersonation of staff to have the 'staff reports' on what exactly had happened in the dining-room yesterday. It turned out to be at a level of 'throwing food at the cooks'; 'mixing mud into the food'. 'We must give some careful thought to how these fifth years should be punished,' I insisted as 'my staff' began

The loss of motivation from a few moments earlier seemed, at least temporarily, to have recovered. Some of the observers commented that the children at this new stage were beginning to be deeply involved. I do not share this interpretation: I recognised the change in some of the class, not as 'involvement' or 'belief' but as a willingness to *work at* involvement and belief: they had not arrived,

98

to tell me the extremes of
retribution to which the
school should resort.

Switch to 'Exercise'
In pairs they were required
to be the fifth years
telling absent friends what
had happened in the dining-
room yesterday – full of joy
in the telling! We finished
the session by finding that the
consensus among the fifth year
had been that they were proud
and boastful of what they
had done.
'Two different attitudes,'
say I, 'to the same incident –
the fifth years' and the
teachers'.'

but were prepared to make
the journey.

Session Two

In the brief gap between the first two sessions, I was aware that for me the drama could be about two things: (1) twelve-year-olds' view of sixteen-year-olds; (2) different perspectives on antisocial behaviour. In fact it never was about (1), although it took some time to dawn on me that (1) provided but the ostensible reason for a twelve-year-old's fantasy trip into committing taboo school and family behaviour. As long as the children and I together continued to refer to 'those sixteen-year-olds' we safely avoided acknowledging that it was themselves that the drama was really about. The drama could only be about (2) in so far as the children were prepared to put a brake on their fantasy trip. In this parti-cular topic – antisocial behaviour related to school – the urge among this age group to fantasise is strong. It is also more easily accessible to collective identification as its context (a class in school) happens to coincide with the one and only context in which the children already exist for each other as a group: a class in school. For a teacher to attempt 'different perspectives on anti-social behaviour' as a learning area, he must anticipate a parti-cularly hightide of unreality, in his terms that is. Whatever structures he adopts must challenge the fantasy stereotyping without denying it. If the tide is too strong he may have to give in to its direction but *not to its formlessness*. The structures must then cater for a change of direction towards reality (if any kind of intellectual growth is to take place) and, failing that, provide a disciplined form for any unyielding expression of highly-charged fantasy.

Action	*Comment*
8 Another factor, perhaps the immediate one, affecting my thinking about the second session was the children's obvious desire to work in small groups 'to show'.	Sometimes one ignores this expectation but I felt these children needed to be made comfortable with what they are good at, so I planned to let them have their heads towards the end of the lesson. I think, however, I made a mistake not to tell them from the beginning what I intended – it might have reduced the apparently frustrated behaviour.
9 Using a length of paper across the floor I invited the class at the beginning of the session to write or draw about things sixteen-year-olds could do that twelve-year-olds couldn't. They worked with interest for a surprisingly long time (about fifteen minutes).	Here I am inviting each individual to choose his own fantasy images.
10 The next move was to give the children the chance to express verbally, in role, some of the things they had drawn and their thoughts on the 'dining-room' incident. So I role-played a reporter 'fishing' for tasty information.	Individual role play was promising but many of the children were by now bored and restless; some were not interested in each other's contributions.
11 Then I put it to them that there could be *five* ringleaders in 5Q and that when we	This was a difficult part of the lesson with some children becoming more destructive

picked them we would look at how their families reacted to the 'incident'.

and nasty to each other and apparently losing whatever faith they had in what I was about and I handled it lamely.

12 Again because there were so many volunteers to be 'the five', I used role play as a means of making a selection, writing on the blackboard any particular attitude that pinpointed differences between the five.

This ploy of 'elevating' what they offer on their feet for examination on the blackboard is useful, but I was careless in the wording, not always using 'second dimension' wording (see Chapter 6) which would have given each ring-leader a more definite peg.

13 I then set up a demonstration between three children of the kind of thing that might be going on in a ring-leader's house.

This was quite successful in that under teacher's questioning the three children could be seen probing for some kind of honest reality. What I could not risk was the use of the popular 'go into your groups and make up a play about each family'. One hopes that their witnessing the raising of standard of thought in the demonstration would then feed into the separate group work which teacher is not then in a position to refine as it takes place.

14 Sorted into groups they start to rehearse. (Can they show "them"? they ask as they move off).

Yes, they indeed showed their competence. Released from teacher they set to to work economically with a strong sense of particularisation to make their scenes come alive.

15 The clock beat them but I promised three things for the next day: they would show something; they would

Knowing there is only one more session I found the pressure on me to round it off to be quite heavy: they would experience being that fifth-year class – in school; they would once more become the staff to decide what to do about 5Q.

have that staff meeting even if they were not ready for it. As it worked out, it became a piece of mistiming to which I resigned myself. This is typical of the teacher's constant dilemma: he cannot always have both roundabouts and swings, and it may be that if he insists on the roundabouts to the neglect of the swings his class will refuse to ride; whereas if he lets them have the swings, they will move to the roundabouts – next time.

Session Three

16 With the children sitting on the floor in front of me (they no longer needed to cling to chairs as they did in the first session), I described to them the three phases that the lesson was to include.

Today they were in a much more co-operative mood, full of anticipation. I think it was a sensible move on my part to share my expectations for the lesson with them from the beginning. They then enjoyed phase one in the knowledge that it would lead to the 5Q experience and phase two, in turn, was coloured by its link with phase three. (I draw the reader's attention to this for in some lessons it is just as important that the class should *not* know what the subsequent phases are to be.)

17 I had already asked some of the children before the lesson started to arrange the chairs chairs formally in five circles, representing the homes of five ring-leaders. I gave them as a focus for this 'showing'

This was disappointingly banal in most cases, not reaching anywhere near the level of the 'demonstration' under teacher's questioning in the second session, even from the three children who had

102

phase that each child would arrive home from school not knowing that the parents had been informed by 'phone of the 'incident'.

In a fairly formal way, linking the scenes by narration, each group briefly enacted the child's reception by his family.

been involved in that particular experience. I would have liked to know whether they felt the drop in standard. One always hopes that children who have been brought up on a diet of small group showing will become self-critical enough to recognise the intrinsic inadequacies of this popular form.

My linking between phase one and phase two was crucial. The level of thinking for the rest of the lesson was to be determined by the children's reaction to what I now had to put to them. I had decided in advance that when they became 5Q I would role play some kind of teacher who would, however reluctantly, be prepared to listen to 5Q's view of their behaviour and who would allow himself to be persuaded by them (if their arguments were good enough) to speak up in their favour at the staff-meeting. By my taking this role the children would be likely to face the following 'contrapuntal' experiences:

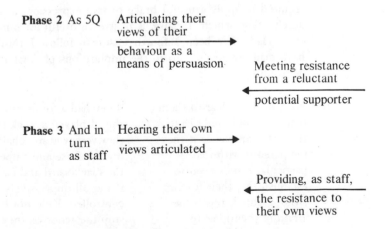

Phase 2 As 5Q   Articulating their views of their behaviour as a means of persuasion

Meeting resistance from a reluctant potential supporter

Phase 3 And in turn as staff   Hearing their own views articulated

Providing, as staff, the resistance to their own views

This typical use of teacher role play was calculated to bring about a change in thinking level – the very achievement my critic was looking for!

There was indeed a change in these children, but not an intellectually receptive one. The change was one of a commitment and energy level not released in the previous two sessions. They were now committed to indulging their fantasies to the full. When I put it to them that before they became 5Q I needed to know from them what kind of teacher I would have to be so that I would eventually be prepared to speak up for them in the staffroom, they, with rising excitement, demanded that I spoke up for them because I was afraid of them!

I have rarely known a teacher's plans for deepening work to recede so quickly! I immediately foresaw that the bottom had fallen out of any intellectual integrity in that staffroom, for now any cogent arguments of support for 5Q would be known to spring from fear not from their validity, so any 'staff' thinking would simply be at an emotive level as there would be no intellectual barrier to counter.

At this point the teacher has a choice of: (*a*) denying the children their fantasy trip; (*b*) letting them have an emotional wallow; (*c*) letting them express themselves emotionally but within some disciplined framework.

To press for the first in these special circumstances would, in my opinion, have been insensitive; to have permitted the second would have been, in my opinion, the worst kind of cathartic indulgence; in my choosing the third the children are required to apply a useful brake to free expression, a deliberate deceleration, which, I claim, is in itself a useful learning experience. Had there been a fourth lesson to follow I think I *must* have made them face up to the implications of what they were demanding.

18 So, I made it clear to them that they could only have their 5Q experience if they tempered it with that particular class's need to establish that their teacher (who, granted, was to be afraid of them) has to understand before he leaves the classroom to go on to the staff meeting the kind of argument he must offer on

They had a lot of fun out of this. I played a weak teacher; they removed my chalk, took my briefcase and tipped over the blackboard and easel, but it was all impressively controlled. I did not have to stop the action as they did not lose sight of the rules of the drama game.

their behalf. In other words,
it could not simply be a
unidimensional 'bash the
teacher' scene – indeed I
would stop the drama if it lost
this required direction.

The staff meeting was held
briefly. The excitement was
high, but the achievement in
terms of quality of thinking
was minimal. Indeed I think
my critic would say harmful,
in that it had reinforced
extremes of stereotype
thinking. At one point I
stopped the staff meeting
because the 'ring-leaders',
in their lemming-like rush to
show their toughness, were
not thinking through the logic
of the scene. They glibly
solved the illogicality but at
least they had been forced to
acknowledge its existence.

The series of lessons finished with a sense, on the part of the teacher, of goals not achieved in terms of intellectual growth and yet other achievements were there that could not be dismissed. There was no doubt that the children, the teacher and many of the observers were feeling satisfied. How dare I, after seven chapters on drama for understanding, now confess to being satisfied with an experience that was conceptually shallow?

Alternative goals

I will now draw on the detailed description of the above lessons in order to put the point that for deepening of understanding to take place certain components must be present; if some of these prerequisites are not readily available and have to be worked for as ends in themselves then the very process of reaching these goals is itself of educational value.

When a topic is selected for or by a group of children or adults their degree of commitment to it and belief in it will be dependent on a mixture of the following factors:

1 *Interest*. The degree of initial interest in the topic.
2 *Collectivity*. The degree to which that initial interest is shared within the group.
3 *Compatibility*. The extent to which the actual emotional network of the class matches the emotional tone and level required by the topic, and is also congruent with their intellectual understanding of the topic.
4 *Effort*. The degree to which they are prepared to work at such emotional or intellectual compatibility, i.e. to work at commitment.
5 *Form*. The degree to which they are prepared to channel their energies released by commitment into some appropriate form.

Each of the above factors will affect how the dramatic material is handled. Inadequacy in any one of them could keep the work within what I referred to earlier as the artificial stage. Let us examine each of them further.

Interest and collectivity

Sometimes a teacher is able to sense a stirring of energy change in a class even as the children or teacher mention a topic. For many secondary teachers of a fourteen-plus age group, however, such a positive response is rare. A row of guarded, impassive faces is what they are more used to, faces of young people whose expectations might be that drama is boring, silly, threatening or irrelevant – or, perhaps nearer the mark, young people whose unspoken, collective agreement puts constraints on any individual aberration from these conventional group attitudes.

It seems to me that there are three broad interest levels that may usefully be distinguished. The first is where subjective feelings are, for some reason, close to the surface. One important factor in the harnessing of this high level of interest is whether or not members of the class share a common reference point. For instance, 'Let's do a play about going to the circus' from a class of children who have recently had a school trip to the circus, or 'Let's do Cowboys and Indians' from a class who have previously done drama about Cowboys and Indians, or 'Let's do the French Revolution' from a class who have together enjoyed *A Tale of Two Cities*, provide very different starting points from those same topics selected by classes who have not had the appropriate group experience. Sometimes, however, one is dealing with dynamite.

Dorothy Heathcote once found herself faced with a request from a group of black and white children in North Carolina to do drama about slavery. Sometimes a teacher stumbles inadvertently on a tricky theme. I recall working with a class of children who had chosen 'immigrants' as their context. I gave them the focus of 'the struggles of an immigrant to find a house', not realising that many of these particular children were slum-clearance children who had just been or were about to be moved from their homes. They tackled the problem of 'what kind of house was right for an immigrant' with a level of energy and zeal that puzzled me until the class teacher explained. Thus when a group of children shares a common problem (being away from home, perhaps, or a compulsory placement in a community home) there is a greater chance of direct transference into the drama experience.

At a less spectacular level there can be, not so much a shared problem, as simply a shared sensational interest: for instance a group of adolescents chose to do their drama about a child murderer because there was dramatic television coverage of such a crime at the time. Similarly with a current circulation of films on the occult a curiosity about black magic can be in the air and find its way into the school drama lessons. It is not unknown for the drama specialist in a comprehensive school to be handling the same fashionable theme with class after class.

Perhaps the most poignant example of group motivation I can recall was in working with a group of adult patients in a psychiatric hospital who, under the skilled direction of John Biroc, Professor of Drama, University of California, re-enacted what it was like to make a suicide attempt – all but one of the group had had this experience. This was an extreme example of *re-education*, but in case the reader, impressed with this illustration, sees himself dabbling in drama as treatment, let me make three important points: (1) it requires someone as mature and sensitive as John Biroc to handle this kind of session; (2) it requires professional backing from the medical and nursing staff; and (3) although there may be times when teachers and therapists share the same goal – evoking insightful behaviour – the starting-point in school is not that the pupils are ill.

A contrasting problem is where the level of interest is mainly intellectual, with little apparent personal experience to draw on; for example, a drama about the poverty of the Third World. For this kind of topic the teacher has to work hard at finding a feeling level that would link the children with the topic, contrasting with the extreme cases at the first level of interest where the teacher has to work hard at *containing* the feeling level.

The third level of interest is characterised by apathy or even antipathy. An example might be where a teacher attempts to use drama to stimulate interest into some A-level literary text which the pupils are already finding obscure and irrelevant.

It seems to me that where the drama succeeds in adjusting an extreme level of interest in a topic, whether it is a toning down of excessive emotional identification or in arousing new feelings about it, it can be regarded as a valid educational experience.

Compatibility

In Chapter 4 we discussed the concept of congruence, that is where the feeling level brought to the fictitious context matches the participants' intellectual understanding of it: 'It is fun to rush for the lifeboats' is an example of lack of congruence. In these cases the children willingly suppress their sense of reality. But another kind of discrepancy is possible: where the children are not *immediately* capable of finding the quality of feeling that belongs to the topic.

Both these discrepancies cropped up in the Riverside

Studio lessons. In Session One, in spite of the twelve-year-olds choosing a topic, violence in school, with a very ready collective reference point, such were the special circumstances of the occasion that feelings such as self-consciousness, embarrassment and apprehension, temporarily overrode the release of emotional energy that would naturally accompany violent action. It is interesting to note that this is where teachers who work solely in Type C drama, Theatre, would not see any problem, for they would invite the children to 'act' violence, thus working from the outside. A better alternative form of activity that can legitimately function independently of a strong feeling level is, of course, Type A, Exercise, i.e. exercise *not* 'folded in' to dramatic playing (see Appendix II).

If some dramatic action is to start the teacher cannot ignore existing strong emotions like embarrassment. Some kind of 'matching' must take place; the fictitious situation need not be about embarrassed characters, but it must give the participants a chance to behave in a subdued, constrained manner likely to contain that embarrassment. Hence the appropriateness of inviting the children who chose violence in school, initially to become the school staff. Similarly, they could have started as the fifth-year form *after* the incident, or a parents' meeting, or an enquiry, anything that did not require those children to *pretend* that they were in an energetic, destructive or revengeful mood. Exactly the same would have applied to a topic that required them to be frightened: a play about the end of the world, or some other 'popular' dramatic crisis that teachers are regularly faced with, like 'house on fire' or 'mountain disaster' or 'shipwreck'.

By Session Three, however, self-consciousness had disappeared and the appropriate energy level was released. The full extent of their subjective feelings the topic aroused could now be expressed in action, so we now faced the opposite kind of danger: that they would lose touch with what they knew intellectually as reality. Thus I had to stop the staffroom scene when, objectively, it appeared not to meet a logic they were fully capable of understanding.

It is unusual to be faced with both problems in the same sequence of lessons but a teacher may well either find himself striving with the first one, especially at upper secondary level where the group determination to remain unmoved precludes an appropriate release of energy even when the class is genuinely interested in the topic, or he may find that an abundance of thoughtless emotional energy continually renders the selected topics meaningless.

If in either of these situations a teacher manages to change the emotional quality of the experience, he will have given his class a worthwhile educational experience.

Effort

If, when once a topic is selected there is not an automatic energy release, then finding the appropriate feeling level is dependent on the pupils' willingness to work at it. The teacher can make it as easy as possible for them by choosing a focus that is in keeping with whatever their actual over-riding mood happens to be as, in the above example, allowing their embarrassment to be contained by a staff-room angle on the violence situation; but the pupils must still, within that focus, voluntarily move the experience in the direction of credibility: that staff meeting must become real enough for the embarrassment to dissipate. This requires a distinct group effort. It is during this phase that the work can most suffer from individual disruptive behaviour; just when the group appears to be committing itself, a strong signal of disbelief from a single member can wreck the chances of a reality being created.

Two common reasons for a class's unwillingness to work is that they are not used to associating drama with work and so resist all effort, or they are more used to a very different format – their expectations are that they will be playing games, or teacher will have a sequence of exercises ready, or they will be allowed to go into small groups rehearsals preparatory to showing each other the results. 'When are we going to do real drama?' might be the thought in their minds even if they do not actually say anything. So the teacher

110

from the very beginning can unwittingly be fighting a resentment that goes with breaking traditions.

Sometimes a teacher can spend a whole lesson or lessons simply getting a group to commit themselves. (It has happened to me more often than I like to admit!) He cannot do it for them. When at last it does take place, no-one can doubt that progress has been made, not simply for the effect on the immediate work, but also, one hopes, that because they have taken the plunge once, diving in a second time will not seem so threatening to them.

Form

The release of emotional energy may be cathartic but it has nothing to do with drama. In some very special circumstances (examples are given on pages 46 and 47) a teacher may tolerate this abuse of the art form, but he must not deceive himself into thinking that the class is working within it. Raw emotion belongs to the actual situation; harnessed, tempered or filtered emotion springs from a dialectic set up between the actual and the fictitious context. Form is made up of the elements that promote and control that interaction: concreteness/abstraction, a sense of time, a sense of significance, contrast and tension. The resulting experience for the participant must be one of heightened self-awareness.

Now it seems to me that where a chosen topic generates a very strong subjective response, the very experience of struggling to express that response within an agreed form is in itself a worthwhile educational experience. (So in these terms the Riverside Studio lessons could be marked 'Satisfactory – just'!) But, more important, is what the children *learn about form itself* in the process of having the experience of it. This is a long-term goal that must play a significant part in guiding a drama teacher's aims and, logically, his criteria for evaluation.

We are now in a position in the next chapter to look at aims more closely. Before we do so let me round off my evaluation of the 'violence in the classroom' lessons.

Potential for learning

No teacher can make children learn; he can only present them with the opportunity. When no conceptual learning takes place, no change in the quality of a class's thinking; it means either that he has failed to provide that opportunity or that the class was not able to take advantage of it. Drama teaching for learning is like a series of moves in chess. An early mistake can affect the whole game: it can spell doom from which one never recovers or it can create no more than a minor setback.

My assessment of Session two at the Riverside Studios is that I made a number of errors of judgement and wrong use of tactics which were, as it happens, not fundamentally destructive. For the most part I claim that teacher-moves in Sessions one and three were productive, and I would probably do exactly the same again. In my own terms and by my own standards I was creating a cognitive/affective learning potential within the material, but for a number of interesting reasons discussed earlier the class was not able to take advantage of it. I claim that they gained from worthwhile, non-intellectual experiences.

The point I want to make here goes beyond my attempt to assess a particular piece of work. I am very concerned to stress the importance of the *potential* for cognitive/affective learning, whether or not it is achieved. For this implies for the participants a central organic structure, a momentum for growth, a reaching forward, an implicit appreciation that 'we are going somewhere'; whatever the material is about, whatever immediate needs we appear to have, whatever skills we are busily acquiring, whatever dramatic playing, exercise or theatrical mode we are in, we sense this purposefulness, this dynamic to which we commit ourselves.

In all my teaching of drama, through drama or with drama, I am ultimately concerned to help children recognise that drama is a dynamic means of gaining new understanding. What I am talking about, therefore, is an attitude in the teacher and in the class towards the 'clay' that they are handling. My hunch over the Riverside experience is that those children sensed new possibilities at their fingertips.

Questions

1 To what extent do you feel the lesson described in this chapter was a failure?
2 Using your own experience illustrate what is meant by 'containing' emotion in drama.

9 Objectives and assessment

I have perhaps now made it clear that above all my aim is to help pupils appreciate drama as a potential for change in understanding; their expectations of this potential being realised provide its necessary dynamic.

Within this overall aim I have a number of objectives, the range of which may now surprise the reader for in the last chapter I began a process of qualifying my position on drama for understanding. I discussed some subsidiary, but not insignificant, educational goals, such as the identifying of group interest; the stimulating or controlling of emotional energy; and the achievement of congruence in response between quality of feeling and intellectual understanding. These are prerequisites rather than goals, but I argued that the very process of working to achieve any one of them provided a learning experience for the participants. I further suggested that the process of harnessing energy and ideas to a dramatic form was an important experience in itself, which in turn provided the opportunity for learning about form. This 'learning about form' becomes my second major objective in drama in education. I shall now attempt to define what this objective means and what its implications are. We are immediately in deep water, for just as aestheticians find it impossible to separate content and form, we shall find that finally we cannot separate the two educational objectives of deepening understanding and 'learning about form': they are mutually dependent.

Learning about form

I have just returned from the county of Avon, where a class selected the well-tried topic of time travel, fixing a date in the future to revisit England. A drama teacher might be for-

114

given for feeling he has been here before! When asked what they thought they might find, one girl, a natural leader of the class, suggested there would be a reverting to primitive ways, where people no longer need machines and were indeed afraid of them because it was thought they housed evil spirits. What rich drama ground lay here! Either this girl had a strong sense of good dramatic material that would immediately takes the class to an examination of values, or she had lifted it straight from television or literature. It is good material, of course, whatever its source.

As soon as the drama started it became very clear that this ten-year-old girl knew how to handle dramatic material: she seemed to sense that there should be significance in every action. As the leader of the 'primitive' people she treated the arrival of strangers from the time machine with a formality of style in both body and speech. But it was her grasp of symbolic meaning within the action that was perhaps even more impressive. When these machine-fearing people were offered a watch as a gift from the strangers, she treated the incident as symbolising the dilemma of two conflicting sets of values. She seemed aware that drama must be concerned with meaning and that carefully selected verbal and non-verbal interaction provided the vehicle for its exploration. She was working towards what Dorothy Heathcote calls a sense of awe.

Along with teacher she was acting as agent, releasing the rest of the class into a high level of dramatic playing. Her supreme ability was as an initiator of dramatic form; in other words, she could manipulate some of its elements of focus, tension, contrast, surprise and symbolisation. Others who could perhaps not be instrumental in this way could nevertheless meet these elements with an appropriate elevated form of behaviour; others again failed to find this heightened (what Dorothy Heathcote calls 'classic') mode: their dramatic playing was naturalistic (what Dorothy Heathcote calls 'domestic'); a few children appeared to be totally bewildered and remained more or less out of the experience.

Our assessment-minded readers might be interested to note the four different levels of achievement here. But does the description imply that this particular girl had reached some final stage in artistic development? In order to answer this satisfactorily we need to look at expressive skills (movement and speech) and autonomy. We will look at the latter first as it sets artistic ability in a context that is peculiarly relevant to drama.

Autonomy

It may occur to the reader that in a book that is loaded with illustrations of teacher-structuring or even manipulation, for the author even to mention autonomy as an objective is an act of self-deception or even dishonesty. My justification lies in the complexity of autonomy as a concept. In drama its achievement cannot be measured without reference to (*a*) its relationship to preceding and subsequent experiences, (*b*) the 'level' of the achievement, and (*c*) closely related to level, the degree to which the autonomy is personal or collective.

Although throughout my work you will find me seeking opportunities for piling more responsibility on the pupils, more often than not it is within a framework decided by me at each stage. Typically I might hand over the reins completely in the final stages of a drama experience. I recall with delight working with some Bristol nine-year-olds on 'Robbing Fort Knox', where, at the beginning of the final lesson, I, in role as the gang leader, had cold feet about the whole project and attempted to call it off at the eleventh hour. The 'gang' took over entirely and the drama rolled on to an exciting climax of group achievement and just retribution over their 'despicable' leader.

Now only in a limited sense can this kind of experience be called autonomy. That it gave the class this responsibility and freedom was more apparent than real, for it was teacher's earlier structuring that had caused it to happen and had also controlled the timing of its happening. Nor must the reader assume that the class, for the next piece of work, would be capable of doing its own structuring towards an equivalent climatic experience.

116

It will be noticed that in both the last two illustrations and others throughout the book I give the class the choice of topic. This is a chance for autonomy at the title and context level, which can leave the teacher firmly holding the reins at more significant levels. In this last Fort Knox example, once I knew their choice of topic I assumed 'gang leadership', immediately selected a second dimension of 'people who have to be meticulous in their reconnaissance and planning', and gathered the children round the blackboard to draw a plan of the fort. In other words I selected a focus that determined the quality of application from the class. Rigidly manipulative? Yes, indeed, but I justify it on the grounds that although, as teacher, I have taken over the instrumental function and by so doing have pitched the level of experience, I have not determined, nor would I wish to determine, what that experience should be. I like the term 'release' into experience for it suggests a freeing, a subjecting of oneself to the dramatic material in one's own way. The narrow boundaries have been drawn by teacher, but the experience is one's own. Significantly, teacher has been the arbiter of that aspect of meaning to be created that is collective, but not personal.

This does not preclude the view that children should become their own agents – in their play they do it all the time. And indeed in some drama lessons they do it all the time. A movement towards autonomy at this level, however, is in my opinion only worthwhile if in cognitive/affective or social terms they can raise the level of the experience for themselves without teacher's help. It seems to me that when children are given a free hand in this way, they either play out at an existential level that has little significance, or their work remains solely instrumental so that they fail to give themselves an 'it's happening to me now' experience at all.

Now quite obviously the girl in the time machine example has reached a high level of sensitivity and is quite capable of acting as an agent, so that the rest of the class had a heightened level of experience. Should this be a teacher's objective for all children? This is where I remain uncertain. Whereas it is fine for the natural leader of the class to take on this function, it would be another matter if several children in the class had this ability.

What exactly is the nature of this ability? It compares with the hyper-awareness that we would like each participant to have of what is happening to him in the dramatic context. But the ability we are now talking about requires an equally sensitive awareness of what is happening to the group as a whole, not only in terms of what is being created collectively, but also what educational benefit individuals appear to be drawing from it.

Even groups of experienced adults (or perhaps especially groups of experienced adults) can fail to be the agents for their own work. It seems very often that the requirement to look at the total happening from the outside denies them the chance of experiencing anything from the inside.

And yet some groups do manage it, just as some actors do manage without a director. If this level of group autonomy is worthwhile then how should we train for it? Here surely an answer is to adopt small group work. (I can visualise the secondary teacher springing to point out to me that such is what most schools do anyway!) By this, however, I do not mean that very popular 'making a statement' drama, but a much more sustained, living-through experience where the adolescents appreciate they are using drama to give themselves a significant experience, which is not necessarily required to meet the criteria of communicability and repeatability.

Indeed the most useful structure I have come across to this end is one that relies on a mixture of whole class and small group activity; for instance, where 'townsfolk' occasionally meet, but are more often in their separate families. Incidentally this same kind of structure is also useful when a teacher wants the children to have a mixture of both Type C, Theatre and Type B, Dramatic playing, where in small groups they *rehearse*, but the 'showing' is logically part of the large group's dramatic playing experience, for example, robbers who have to 'prove' themselves by enacting the most dangerous 'job' they have ever tackled (nine-year-olds) or re-enacting (after rehearsal) before a primitive court of law each group's version of how the king met his death (adolescents).

In case I am misleading readers, let me also say that I think there are times when 'making a statement' drama can be very valuable; I am against its use at the *expense* of a living-through experience. One big advantage of 'making a statement' drama, of course, is that it does meet the objective of autonomy. As the reader will realise, Type D, Drama for understanding, like Type C, Theatre tends to be dependent on the leader.

Language

Expressive skills in drama, speech and movement have for many years been the keystone of many different kinds of drama syllabuses, for all ages. Many teachers, threatened by the vagueness and apparent goal-lessness of such activities as improvisation, seize the chance to train children in these verbal and non-verbal forms of communication for both their obvious intrinsic value and their amenability to training schemes.

Expressive skills, however, must be seen within the larger context to which they clearly belong: language. Hence the title of this section. Many recent educational publications claim an important relationship between drama and the acquisition of language skills, including communication skills, but I would like to go further than this by suggesting that in many ways drama *is* language, and that although I have barely mentioned the topic in preceding chapters I have implicitly been discussing language all the time. It is as if drama is a cobweb and language its strands: you cannot conceive of one without the other.

I am talking about language in its very broadest sense of course, as a non-verbal/verbal code for encapsulating and sharing experience. It is a currency for handling meaning. A powerful example occurred in the time machine illustration. The 'primitive' people received three distinct signals of meaning:

1 A small group of us, leaving our time machine, approached the wary inhabitants, who hurriedly retreated at the sight of us.
2 After a quick consultation among ourselves we sent one representative forward.
3 Encouraged by the success of this we offered a present – a watch.

Now we have in these three moves one of the principal functions of language – the signalling of subjective intentions in a form that can have objective meaning, which for the inhabitants was interpreted as hostile: a group approaching; neutral; an individual approaching; and friendly; a present offered.

'Stop! Do not touch that present – it is a machine' was the command from our ten-year-old girl for whom the non-verbal symbols were suddenly inadequate. Apart from extending the form of the signalling she has now adopted three other functions of language:

1 *Controlling*. Language in dramatic playing, as in life, is our chief medium for making things happen.

2 *Role-defining*. She used language to give herself the status of leadership.

3. *Changing the level of meaning*. This needs some explaining.

She switched to spoken language in order to look at implications and consequences of events, but because of the pre-agreed attitudes to machines she has also opened the door, just an inch or so, towards an abstract discussion of conflicting values. (It only requires one child to ask why and she could find herself attempting to articulate abstractions barely within her grasp. Indeed, although she was not so challenged immediately, it was astonishing how towards the end of the second session several children were working very hard to communicate at that high level.) The important thing to stress here, however, is that this flight into a level of abstract thinking has sprung from a concrete base of here and now actuality. This once again draws our attention to the particular power of the dramatic medium: its highest abstractions are tethered to the here and now of action. 'Do not touch that present' could not be more secure in its concrete action base and yet it can release into both proposition and poetry. Indeed it must move away from, but never lose touch with, its base if it is to become part of a form that is both artistic and educational.

Other functions of language in drama will be recognised as educationally invaluable:

1 *Practice in the language of hypothesis.* The problem-solving feature of much drama allows opportunities of this kind. 'How would the wicked bears persuade sensible Snow White to leave the house?' ask the six-year-old Dwarfs. 'In what circumstances might an inner-city plague caused by rats reach a village two hundred miles away where there were no rats?' was the question facing a class of nine- to eleven-year-olds about to enact the story of Eyam in Derbyshire.

2 *Practice in roles.* In some ways all language learning can be said to be an experimentation in roles (I am using the term sociologically here). Perhaps one of the most obvious uses of drama is that it can artificially (and safely) contrive all kinds of role experience that can break historical, cultural, class, race and generation barriers. It can also cut across the normal language code (in Bernstein's terminology). Particularly evident in drama is the opportunity a teacher has for working safely in those very modes of communication where people are normally most vulnerable, where working-class participants, normally protected by the communally employed 'condensed' symbol, can be challenged to individualise the articulation of their ideas, or where middle-class participants, normally protected by their habit of using language independent of context, can be challenged to get in touch with their feelings.

3 *Awareness.* 'How can I see what I think till I hear what I say?' asks Alice in Wonderland. It is probably true that we find out more about ourselves in the face-to-face interaction of discourse. As Berger and Luckmann (1972) have put it: '... as I objectivate my own being by means of language, my own being becomes massively and continuously available to

myself at the same time that it is so available to him, and I can spontaneously respond to it without the "interruption of deliberate reflection".' Again drama is unique in that its discourse is undertaken within a sharpened focus and with a balance of affect and cognition that is self-exposing.

4 *Cognition.* Wilkinson (1971) quotes the observation: 'The meaning of deprivation is a deprivation of meaning (p. 109). Drama appears to offer qualities and levels of meaning not normally available to children in anything but an abstract form. Just as in the classic case of Whorf's (1966) Eskimos' perception of snow, within novel drama situations (offering experience novel to the participants that is), new subtle distinctions may be drawn which become encapsulated in an extended vocabulary.

5 *Style.* Language allows the child through drama to call forth the whole world into the here and now at the drop of a phrase. Part of the meaning of that phrase is its style, a style that can be poetic, heroic, primitive, scientific, technological, ecclesiastical, legal, martial and personal. Appropriate delivery of speech and gesture to accompany that phrase is a very useful means of extending its meaning.

So we are back to expressive skills! Yes, they are important goals. I hope this section has placed them in a larger language perspective, indicating areas of learning that appear to be more important for some children than the mode of communication. Much teaching of speech (and its subsequent assessment) is still tackled from the outside; the externals of the activity are trained and tested. It may be, like Portia's caskets, the more important things are going on inside.

Reading and writing

Drama that is experience rather than skill-oriented is a powerful way of helping children grasp the conception of words on paper as codes signalling experience. Dorothy Heathcote in England and David Booth in Canada have done a great deal of interesting work in this area, the former mainly with adolescents who have been 'turned off' difficult scripts, the latter with young children who can read mechanically, but do not comprehend.

It is ironical that at the time of writing this book there is an educational trend 'back to basics'. Infant teachers tell me that they have no time for drama as they must raise the standard of reading and writing. So they drop the very tool that would help them!

There is a wide range of reading and writing activities that can be structured within the drama experience. Whether it is the examination of historical documents which various forms of 'hypothesising' role play will help 'crack' (John Fines and Ray Verrier, 1974, have done exciting work in this direction), or writing letters to be smuggled out of the Tower, or a class of infants struggling to decipher a crucial message that has some words missing, or ESN children finding their own words printed and looking like a book, or a group of Canadian adolescents capturing the mood of rural life in nineteenth-century England in order to cope with Thomas Hardy (this is followed up in Wagner, 1976): the key to it all rests in the unique availability of experience that drama can bring to a classroom just as it is required.

Social skills

As objectives social skills, social interaction or interpersonal behaviour, rate very high on syllabuses for drama throughout the country. Some teachers have improvement of the social health of the class as the only goal for their lessons, their argument being that drama provides the only opportunity on the timetable for this kind of development.

Very few people would quarrel with the view that social development is an area neglected by our schools and that drama is a useful vehicle to this end. I do, however, have doubts in two respects: I am not sure that I can accept some current practice that appears to connive at a low-level standard of drama on the grounds that the all important social needs are being met; and it seems to me that it should be a rare occurrence for social improvement to be the only goal when clearly sensible structuring could concurrently meet a number of additional requirements related to meaning, language and aesthetic form.

A distinction also needs to be drawn between social learning that is intrinsic to the drama and that which is extrinsic. The examples I gave on pages 70–71, where I work with the psychiatric adult patients for the purpose of getting them to examine their own social skills within a variety of contexts, I would regard as intrinsic, where the drama itself is illuminating social behaviour. But often there is social benefit almost as a bonus to the drama activity, where the sheer task of working together on anything creative happens also to be socially productive. Most of my drama work tends to be in this latter category where any social learning is extrinsic to the experience itself.

I think it is fairly common for teachers to adopt social goals for particular pupils in the class, pupils who create problems for their peers by overdominating, isolates who create problems for themselves, or scapegoats for whom drama can be just another subtle means of victimisation.

It is very important that the teacher should make himself aware as soon as possible of the social network of his classes especially where the dramatic activity is likely to reinforce antisocial attitudes and behaviour. I recall vividly working with a class of sixteen- to eighteen-year-olds who felt very threatened by an intelligent, articulate member of the group, so the only way of coping was to 'kill her off' – quite legitimately within the rules of the dramatic context.

This raises the question of the wisdom of bringing into the open with a class the problem of its own social ill-health. In the instance I have just cited I felt it was very important for the girl and for the class to admit to themselves what was happening, that there could be no growth for that group until the matter was honestly discussed. Indeed for some drama exponents (David Clegg is a good example), the main purpose of doing drama is to create opportunities for explicit discussion of this kind.

Personally I am much more concerned first to apply the

two criteria of whether the group dynamics is blocking, undermining or limiting the dramatic activity, and whether the group appear to be ready to cope with this degree of exposure. It could be, of course, that my advice on this is guided by cowardice rather than wisdom!

In talking about 'the group', the leader is part of it. I often catch myself arrogantly detecting weaknesses in the dynamics of the group I am working with without acknowledging that my contribution should be included in the diagnosis. Recently I asked four adults, all with a drama reputation (an adviser, a college of education lecturer, an advisory teacher and a teacher), who knew each other quite well but who had never before been required to participate in practical drama with each other or with me, to set up an improvisation on terms dictated by me. Their planning would be listened to by me; the improvisation would be watched by me. The 'blocking' tactics employed by the group to delay starting were classical! And can one wonder? It did lead, however, to quite a useful, simple analysis of the different levels that consistently operate in improvisation work. You will see from the following table how group dynamics, like the unwelcome guest, cannot be ignored.

The improvisation was about a father who had let the side down by 'grassing'. His criminal family remained loyal to him and shared the anxiety of wondering whether the gang yet knew. The levels of experience, as we have indicated before, fall into two categories of the fictitious and the real. The total experience is dependent upon the dialectic set up between these two categories. Their elements might be listed as follows:

Levels of meaning in an improvisation

FICTITIOUS — *what is being created.*

1 PLOT	about a man who 'grassed'.
2 CONTEXT	a family of criminals living in a London high-rise flat at a certain time of day.
3 THEME	waiting for news.
	the effect on three other members of the family.

125

4 Spontaneous meanings that emerge, e.g. conflict between father and son.

ACTUAL – *the experience of creating.*
1 The conscious effort (or lack of it!) of the four participants to meet the requirements of the task.
2 Group interaction. To a large extent the meaning of the experience is controlled by the established pattern of group dynamics. In this case between four personalities – and a fifth with a large measure of authority over the whole proceedings.
3 Personal 'luggage' – drawing on past experiences in order to create the fictitious level.
Personal 'pressure' – from the task, from the tutor, from the group.
Personal meaning (significant or insignificant) found within the task, either in what you find yourself contributing or in what you receive from the experience.
Personal reflection after the task is completed.
The last item on the above list of levels of meaning is a requirement that needs further attention.

Reflection
Experience in itself is neither productive nor unproductive; it is how you reflect on it that makes it significant or not – significant for good or ill, of course.

It seems to me there are three kinds of reflection: (1) personal, (2) universal and (3) analogous. The first is obviously a change in self-awareness: as a result of an experience (including dramatic experience) a person has gained insight into his own psychological make-up or into the social environment in which he lives. The second is the conscious placing of an experience within a higher level of abstraction, a movement from the particular to a generalised theory or principle. 'Things aren't always what they seem' might be the reflective conclusion of the five-year-olds who in their drama drank some liquid because it was an interesting colour. The third kind of reflection makes a leap from the drama context to another context. An impressive example for me occurred in the incident I mentioned earlier in this chapter of the sixteen- to eighteen-year-olds 'killing off' the girl to whom they had taken a dislike. Still within the drama they then proceeded with some cunning to 'cover-up' the cause of her death. This drama was actually taking place in July 1974 in Canada, at the time of the Watergate trials!

It seems to me that the timing of the reflection is crucial to its effectiveness. Routine teacher/class discussions immediately after the dramatic event are not always the most helpful. Perhaps the most powerful form is the reflection that goes on at the same time as the drama, that is from within the drama, so that as things are happening, and as words are spoken, their implications and applications can be articulated legitimately as part of the drama itself.

When the reflection takes place after the drama its promotion may depend on the teacher's sensitivity to what the experience has really been about for the participants. So often I have found myself discussing the wrong points or making the wrong references because I have been wrapped up in what I *wanted* the experience to be about. The primary school teacher meeting the class every day has an enormous advantage in this respect over the drama specialist in a secondary or middle school, for the timing of referring to the drama, or the ripe opportunity to do so, may be dependent on something relevant cropping up the next day or the day after, or even a couple of weeks after the drama experience. This seizing of an opportunity to link new material with the drama experience is not available to the drama specialist, who has to accept the frustration that he will not even see the class again until next week. (This does not apply to American and Canadian schools; but in England we still assume that dramatic creativity is something to be switched on once a week, in some cases, just for thirty-five minutes.)

Performance skills and theatre crafts

The Type D drama, Drama for understanding, teacher will not necessarily have performance skills as objectives at all. It seems to me that whereas one could argue the case for all pupils of all ages to practise the use of drama in one form or another, one would be hard put to justify training all children as performers.

Nevertheless some children can gain a great deal from performance opportunities. Even as I say this I am aware that I shall be quoted and subsequently misconstrued by readers who want to have a blessing given to actor-training as part of the drama curriculum. I am aware too that anything that appears to perpetuate the educationally shallow theatre performances that go on once or twice a year for the benefit of teachers who do not know any better and for their children's parents who like their offsprings' 'shown off' on stage (and TV if you are lucky) could be regarded as a risk not worth taking. But as I have seen just as bad non-performance drama as I have performance drama it seems to me that we are taking risks in promoting any kind of drama. In this section I examine more closely the notion of 'showing' so that any judgement about performance can be made against some kind of theoretical framework.

Drama is metaphor. Its meaning lies not in the actual context nor in the fictitious one, but in the dialectic set up between the two. Many of the essential characteristics of drama are to be found in child play and it is still useful to illustrate from this least sophisticated form, partly for its relative simplicity but also because it provides us with a conception that is the converse of theatre.

Let us examine its principal characteristics. When a child plays being a policeman, he is creating a meaning in action from the juxtaposition of himself and whatever he knows about policeman. The purpose is some kind of private self-satisfaction. The direction of his energies could be said to be intrapersonal. The mode of the activity is a mixture of instrumental and existential: 'I am making it happen so that it can happen to me.'

Now supposing the child, during his play, switches to saying 'Look at me Mummy; I am a policeman,' what difference does it make? First let us take note of the function of the phrase 'I am a policeman'. The child through this use of language has attempted to make 'public' what had been

128

a private experience. The purpose is objectification of experience. The language form itself is not metaphor but the language of explanation. Now what is significant here is the effect on the subsequent make-believe action. If his purpose is now to *show* his policeman experience to his mother *he must find the action equivalent to 'public' verbal language*, in other words the action which in its language form must take on the function of explanation. Just as 'I am a policeman' labelled experience but was not itself the experience, so his action will now have a labelling function but will not be the experience. The mode, because of the new *extra*-personal direction, will be rendered less significant in its existential aspect. (Rather as the vacuum salesman, for whom the experience in itself of cleaning the carpet is not important, nevertheless does so with gusto.) Whatever he was enjoying, acquiring or learning from the first experience is replaced by a new experience with a new set of (not unimportant) satisfactions. To an unaware observer it might look like a repetition of the same experience. Let us tabulate our assertions:

	Child playing	*'Look at me'*
Purpose	Self-satisfaction	Objectification
Direction	Intra-personal	Extra-personal
'Language' form of action	Metaphor (private)	Explanation (public)
Mode	Instrumental/existential	Instrumental

These then appear to be the four main dimensions: purpose, direction, language form, and mode. But what happens when two children play together, sharing their make-believe, with no-one watching. The tables might be contrasted as follows:

	One child	*Two children*	*'Look at me'*
Purpose	Self-satisfaction (subjective)	Mutual satisfaction (mainly subjective)	Objectification

Direction	Intra-personal	Interpersonal	Extra-personal
'Language' form of action	Metaphor (private)	Metaphor and explanation	Explanation (public)
Mode	Instrumental/ existential	Instrumental/ existential	Instrumental

The temptation now is to claim that Type B and D drama coincide with the middle column and Type C with the 'Look at me' column. This is helpful only if the reader bears in mind that we are talking about an activity that is so complex that categorising in this way oversimplifies. The above classifications meet the requirements of logic rather than practice. What appears to be valid is that in Type D drama the four dimensions can be used in significantly varied ways. Extremes of these differences are more marked in switching from, say, Type B to Type C, but in practice there can be a large measure of variation within the same type. What also appears to be valid is the claim that whereas Types B and D orientate towards existential experience, Type C veers towards explanation, statement or demonstration – the difference in fact between a child absorbed in 'being a policeman' and explaining or showing that he is one.

But is one a less valuable experience than the other? Having an experience and finding a public form in which to encapsulate it seem to me to have significance. But supposing the child *learns to make a public statement not from his own experience but from models of other public statements?*

Here we have reached the central issue in all school theatre performances. It is not that public showing (whether it is with other groups in the class, other teachers, the class next door, parents, or an audience of strangers) is itself educationally invalid (indeed in many cases the opposite is true) but that so often children of all ages seem to be required to share with an audience someone else's encapsulation of experience, whether it be a Nativity story, a teacher's or Shakespeare's script.

Much theatre in school starts from this false position of making explicit what has never been implicit, of externalising what has never been internalised. This can apply even where the theatre performance has come 'from their own ideas' for unless their rehearsing allows them to explore and investigate and learn more about the nature of their own ideas, before becoming re-encapsulated in the action of performance, what they will offer their audience is an active representation of concepts or stories that have little experiential foundation.

It seems possible that children of all ages can gain from the dramatic equivalent of the child's 'Watch me, Mummy' if it has grown from a worthwhile experience in the first place. This does not preclude the interpretation of texts, provided the text is used initially as a springboard to open up significant new experience for the pupils. (I have discussed this aspect more fully in an article in *Young Drama* [Bolton 1978].)

Satisfaction

Whatever long- or short-term objectives a teacher may have, it seems to me that 'satisfaction' must be included. This is to be distinguished from 'enjoyment', which many teachers seem to put as a priority; there is an assumption which I mentioned earlier that if the pupils have enjoyed their drama that is evidence enough of its educational validity. Many children are taught that drama should be 'fun' and often measure its success in those terms. 'Satisfaction' on the other hand equates it with all other school activities where, one hopes, the rewards come from hard work and the acquisition of knowledge and skills.

Assessment

In view of the wide range of aims and objectives that have now appeared, it seems not unreasonable for anyone who is asked how he assesses the work to throw the question back at the questioner: 'Which aspect of the work are you asking about?' For we now have quite a lengthy list of possible alternatives:

Overall aims
Change in understanding
An expectation of change in understanding as a primary
  purpose
Satisfaction from and understanding of the art form.

Objectives
Autonomy
Language development including expressive skills
Social skills
Theatre skills
Reflection.

Prerequisites
Identification of group interests
Stimulation/control of group energy
Commitment
Congruence
Finding a dramatic form.

I am not sure how useful it is to classify in this way. What
I want to establish is that nothing can be achieved unless the
elements in the prerequisite list are present and that the aims
list distinguishes fundamental priorities over the objectives.
However, in any one lesson a teacher could be structuring the
work towards prerequisites, objectives and aims simultaneously.

There appear to be four kinds of assessment: (1) assessment of the teacher (self or observer assessment); (2) assessment of the work; (3) assessment of pupil progress; and
(4) assessment of achievement.

1 Assessment of the teacher
The following questions can usefully be asked of the teacher,
either by himself or by an observer:
(*a*) What is this teacher's reading of the wants and needs of
   the class?
(*b*) Does that reading seem reasonable?
(*c*) What objectives has he selected?
(*d*) Are those objectives realistic?
(*e*) Can he articulate and justify his selection of objectives

for *this lesson* – as opposed to vague broad aims like the popular 'improving their social health'?

(*f*) What strategies has he selected in his planning?

(*g*) Are they appropriate, effective? (For instance, does a particular strategy meet more than one objective at the same time?) Have they the potential for tapping meanings *beyond* the explicit?

(*h*) How aware is he of the 'play for them'? Does he *really* see and listen?

(*i*) To what degree is he able to adapt his preparation to 'their play' as it emerges or, alternatively, to what extent is he able (and justified) to limit the pupils' autonomy for the sake of his objectives without spoiling their satisfaction?

(*j*) To what extent can he recognise and see new openings, thus discarding his prepared objectives for the sake of alternatives that are for some reason: (i) more worthwhile; or (ii) more immediate?

(*k*) Do his thinking on his feet, his use of his voice and body, his selection of signals, his handling of strategies, his switching from dramatic action to reflection and back again, his sense of timing, his choice of teaching register, his selection of symbols, all have coherence and integrity within the total experience?

(*l*) How realistic is his own assessment immediately after and some time after the lesson?

2 Assessment of the work

Who is doing the assessing? Headmasters and others need to be satisfied that the drama in their schools is, to use R.S. Peters's term, *worthwhile*. The answer to this depends largely on the perspective of the person making a judgement: some people expect to observe an improvement in skills, others a group awareness; some CSE and GCE syllabuses see a knowledge of theatre studies as an ultimate goal.

The Type D drama teacher is in a difficulty in that his two major aims of change of understanding, which is to do with values, and satisfaction from and understanding of the art form, are not behaviours that can be tested.

133

Additionally 'worthwhileness' in terms of change of understanding depends on the views of the observer. We have not so far in this book faced the uncomfortable fact that change of understanding in itself cannot automatically be of value. Change to understanding *what*? And who decides? Whether we like it or not the drama teacher is faced with a moral dilemma. Drama is a powerful medium for change in his hands. Is it his own or society's values that he is to inculcate? If he believes that society is corrupt is that what he is to teach?

Or is there a less specific alternative? Is it possible to steer a course that does not come down in support of any particular view but causes children to examine and re-examine their own views and values? It seems possible that by drama for understanding we mean a constant enlarging or shifting of perspective so that the participants have to reassess their current understanding. Even this neutral position will worry many teachers who do not want their pupils consciously to go through a process of appraisal. Indeed they might argue that this continual inspection of long-standing values by children who are not old enough to know what they are about leads to unnecessary unrest and dissatisfaction.

Obviously each teacher must make up his own mind on this. He must decide whether, for example, it is legitimate to use drama to criticise the Russian government's use of psychiatric hospitals for political agitators, the South African's promotion of apartheid, the British expulsion of the Banaban people, the Canadian treatment of their indigenous populations or the Australian treatment of the Arnhem aborigines, or alternatively to teach a generalisation, using a fictitious context to do so, that people, and their governments, with vested interests tend to shift their normal position of integrity. Or he may opt to avoid issues that have this kind of moral or political or religious bite. But what does he do if he is, say, an anti-abortionist, and his adolescent class in choosing the topic for their improvised drama clearly show that they are in favour? And what further does he do if their solution, because it happens to be a school in Britain, is backed by the law, or, because the school happens to be in Canada, is against the law?

I have no solution to these problems. I tend to use drama in a way that poses questions, rather than implies answers (although one must bear in mind that the fact that a teacher often indicates the questions is itself a non-neutral position to take); if I am working in a country other than my own I avoid topics that happen to be political hot-potatoes, and in my own country out of respect for the school I am working in I tend, if possible, to avoid topics I know the school would not consider proper or that could be misconstrued. I am probably more careful than I would be if I were a member of a school staff, where I would be in a much stronger position to know more fully the nature of the risk.

What causes me great concern is that these issues can arouse a fervour of shocked protest. If only that degree of concern could be harnessed in opposition to the lemming-like rush to the trivial! For the major problem in drama in this country is not that basic values are being challenged, but that nothing is being challenged at all.

This brings us to another important point in discussing the activity's worthiness. Given that some significant change in understanding is achieved through the drama, this can only be approved as worthwhile if it passes a further test: application. Unless some kind of adaptation takes place out of the drama lesson context the drama cannot be said to be effective. I am often aware, in working with psychiatric patients, that improved insight into their own problem does not of itself provide them with the means of doing anything about it. In school, of course, we are not normally dealing with personal problems, so that any application of what is learnt cannot be followed through as in psychiatric work. Often we have blind faith in the efficacy of our drama work in relation to its central aim. Other objectives like communication skills and social behaviour are perhaps more easily observable and certainly achievement of the pre-requisites is easily discernible.

3 Assessment of pupil progress
I have suggested that ultimately achievement in understanding and its application require an act of faith on the part

of the teacher, but pupils often give clues that are worth noting here of some kind of affective/cognitive change. Perhaps the most noticeable is the way a pupil reflects on his experience, especially when it takes place in role within the drama. Another clue is the degree of ease with which he generalises from the experience or draws upon parallels to it. Often a desire to talk about what has happened is an indication of the intensity of the experience. Another guide is his quality of performance in related arts (drawing, and particularly poetry) subsequent to the experience – expressing a desire to encapsulate the dramatic experience in another non-discursive form.

These are all clues to a particular meaningful experience, but there are also changes in behaviour that can usefully be observed over a period of time, changes that indicate progress in a pupil's competence in dramatic activity. These changes can be classified as follows:

(*a*) Attitude towards; expectations of drama.

(*b*) Amount of effort, especially during an unrewarding phase.

(*c*) Integrity of feeling.

(*d*) Intellectual grasp of what is being created by whole group.

(*e*) Sensitivity to the needs of others within the group.

(*f*) Ability to select action and words that enhance the significance of the experience for oneself and for others, and, conversely, to *receive* from others.

(*g*) Ability to work economically both in and out of the drama.

(*h*) An awareness of form, particularly in terms of selecting or retaining focus and injecting or sustaining tension.

(*i*) An openness to symbolic meaning.

(*j*) Role identification.

(*k*) Readiness and ability to evaluate and reflect on the work and his own contribution to it.

(*l*) Willingness to take risks, to try new territory, new forms.

(*m*) Trust in the teacher; readiness to evaluate and criticise the teacher's contribution.

The children in a particular class may be at the bottom rung of most of these ladders, so that progress implies simply moving up a single step. Indeed the teacher who is struggling to get a class onto the first rung of (*a*) is not likely to find that any of the other categories are relevant. When he *does* succeed in this direction he quite rightly feels the class has made a leap forward, although a visitor might wonder at what he had to be pleased about. For the visitor might have some notion about standards, which brings us to the next section.

4 Assessment of achievement

Presumably the most able ideal pupil in drama has reached the top of all the above ladders. How old does the reader assume this pupil is? Are there in fact certain developmental phases in drama that would neatly allow us to point to the equivalent of perspective in art or of singing in tune in music? One could claim that in the young child the acquisition of 'perspective' in drama might be his ability to share his make-believe with another child and eventually a larger class and that in older children the ability to interpret a text, make a theatrical statement, and handle the crafts of theatre are criteria of development, but the former is peculiar to a whole range of social contexts and the latter applies only to a one-sided aspect of drama in schools.

It seems to me that it is, in theory at any rate, possible for a seven-year-old child to meet the requirements of (*a*) to (*m*) above, for they are requirements dependent in the main on factors *other than drama*. So whatever would count towards a considered opinion that this child was a mature seven-year-old would also count in his ability to conduct himself in dramatic activity. In fact I have met many seven-year-olds who are far better at drama than children twice their age. This is not as surprising as it may seem for good drama requires that the participants bring their whole selves, their honest selves, their commitment, their willingness to observe themselves or to learn from experience. All these things are too painful for many young adolescents, who are often at a developmental stage that can be insecure if not bewildering. The last thing they are going to attempt is an artistic activity that is self-exposing.

So in a peculiar way ability in drama is tied, not to an achievement level in drama as such, but to personal maturity. This makes it extraordinarily difficult for CSE moderators, who are really attempting to assess the maturity of the participants, what they are like as people. They will, of course, attempt to cloak their discussion in terms of apparent drama skills but as these skills are controlled by personal development it is impossible for an assessor to make a useful distinction.

A friend of mine who is Head of a comprehensive school English and Drama Department recently remarked that anyone who is given a Grade I for CSE Drama must be an exceptional *person*. He added that if only employers would recognise this they could guarantee themselves first-class employees. He was not joking; he meant it. But he would add that far from personal development controlling the drama, the drama enhances personal development, which is exactly what Brian Way (1967) has been telling us for years!

The possibility is too strong to ignore that continual opportunity to exercise skills along the (*a*) to (*m*) dimensions is itself a maturing process. The theoretical framework of this book does not allow for anything as vague as this and I am not happy to include an 'umbrella' aim of this kind but I think we cannot deny what Brian Way and Peter Slade (1954) before him grasped as a central aim of drama in education that it is concerned with the development of the person, that it enhances the natural maturation process.

Questions

1 Which do you consider to be the most important section of this chapter?
2 There is only one more chapter left in this book. What topics do you feel it should include and why?

10   Teacher's thinking

This final chapter provides a way of summarising the main points that the book has attempted to discuss. By looking at what might go on in a teacher's head we are really giving ourselves a second chance to look at some of the principles.

There is no doubt that a successful drama teacher must be a flexible thinker, often being required to promote a mode of thought differing from that of the class, in order to enrich the class's thinking: if the class thinks in story-line, he will think situationally; if the class thinks in conceptual hierarchies, he will think in values; if the class errs towards the abstract, he will move towards the concrete; if they stay with the functional, he will emphasise the universal. So let us see what all this means in practical terms.

Situation v. Story

For a long time drama has been associated with telling a story. Children themselves will usually be concerned, as they dramatise, with 'What happens next?' or 'What can we make happen next?' Now dramatic form is essentially concerned with the present. As Susanne Langer (1953) puts it, it is a present 'filled with its own future' but its interest does not centre on moving out of the present into the future, but in staying with the present in order to examine it. This is what I mean by 'situational'.

So one aspect of the teacher's thinking is how to turn what appears to the children to be a rapid sequence of events into an examination of the present. It means that waiting for Grendel to arrive must be significant in itself; the process of coming to a decision to leave a rural cottage in the eighteenth century for an industrial city must be more important than the leaving, and in turn the departure must be more important than the journey, and so on. Each is a series of presents steeped in significance.

In practice, therefore, the children may say, 'We'll be scientists who build a monster to destroy the world' – and building the monster – with all it requires in the way of reference books, technology, step-by-step decisions, blueprints and test-trials, takes up the next three hours of drama. By the time they are ready to destroy the world they have had time to weigh up the implications of what they are doing. If after all this time they still opt for destruction then that is too bad, but at least they have had to justify their decision. The children may say 'a play about a tidal wave' – the wave comes in the fifth lesson! I recently attempted to 'do' the Plague of Eyam in one lesson. One feature of this badly-handled drama experience was that I never allowed the children to find the reality of a present time. As teacher I was caught up in the 'what should happen next' syndrome: 'a stranger would arrive . . .' and then 'he would contaminate the village . . .' and then 'someone will die . . .' and then 'we'll have a meeting about not leaving our village' etc. In other words I fell into the very trap of which I am trying to warn others.

This anecdote brings home very sharply the difficulty which must somehow be surmounted in doing drama about a known sequence, as in history or a known story from literature. The temptation here to be content to use drama as narrative, to tell a story, is very strong, for the story form is already known to the participants and as such appears to be more amenable to presentation than to exploration. To think situationally within a story, therefore, often requires a teacher to work indirectly or obliquely to the story itself: for the participants to experience the town of Hamelin bereft of children after the Pied Piper has left; to experience the guilty return home by Jacob's sons after they have sold Joseph their brother to the Egyptian merchants; to experience the conflict of professional and personal conscience as Creon's soldiers, forbidden to allow the burying of the dead; to experience the conspiratorial planning for mutiny before

Columbus sights land.

But when a drama is over there can be pleasure in looking back on the story created. Very occasionally one finds oneself deliberately manipulating a plot in order to meet an educational objective. The most striking incident for me was in a third lesson on 'Outlaws' (video-taped by the Inner London Education Authority) with a class of ten-year-olds, where in order to raise the status of the girls who had in the first two lessons been fading by the side of the dynamic personalities of the boys, I was driven to use plot as a way of making us dependent on the girls. (And since I have mentioned this particular occasion, my handling of which has proved somewhat controversial, may I emphasise that I believe that raising someone's status is usually achieved, not by supporting with cushions, but by challenging with hurdles.)

However, for a teacher to think in plot terms is usually misguided. Sometimes, because of their training in drama, teachers become plot dependent in their planning of lessons. Even where the story is not previously known, they will start building one, thinking that that is what lesson preparation is. Compare the following types of thinking:

Plan A

1 The chief of the tribe has died mysteriously.
2 A scene where cause of death is investigated.
3 Someone is accused of murder.
4 A tribal trial scene.
5 Execution scene.

Plan B

The chief of the tribe has died mysteriously.

The situation must open up the experience (depending on what the class is ready for and capable of coping with) of:

(*a*) Spreading or coping with rumour (the most superficial level).

or

(*b*) Not knowing who you can trust; subtly testing.

or

(*c*) A cover-up.

or

(*d*) Living with the shock of the sudden removal of security (the most sophisticated level).

Whichever of the above experiences in Plan B he chooses, the teacher knows it will depend on a very slow build-up of meaning, with much checking (either from outside or inside in drama) on the normal values of that tribe. Perhaps it would become necessary to go back in time to find out the nature of relationships with the chief or what it was like when the *status quo* was unthreatened. Whatever 'movement' there is within the experience it will be towards an enhancement of selected meaning. Plan A, however, is bound to a single movement from event to event. Of course with Plan B something recognisable as plot will emerge; it may well be that a scene investigating the cause of death takes place, but again if it does it is because it appears to be a potentially productive situation in terms of meaning: consequences from the past and implications for the future.

The conflict between a teacher's thinking and that of his class can sometimes be frustrating and, fortunately, amusing. So the teacher can find himself grandly in role announcing 'In all the winters I have known, the ice on our stream has never been so thick. It's like a rock. Not even our heaviest axe can make a single dent' – teacher all set for 'a caveman's longest winter ever' situation when a fellow caveman shrieks, 'I've cracked it,' and others: 'And I have; I have; me too,' and, finally, 'I've made a big hole!'

Categorising

Most topics suggested by a class can be split up into various aspects, for instance:

War: fighting; strategies; training; prisoners; shortage; civilians; soldiers.

Ships: design; building; safety; crew; passengers; navigation.

Florence Nightingale: Scutari hospital; training; nurses; patients; doctors; battles; journey.

These are examples of aspects which in turn could all be

broken down into further categories. Thus, under 'Ships', crew could be subdivided into officers and men; work and leave; clean jobs and dirty jobs; sailing ship and steam ship. All these are objective conceptual classifications of a kind that do not bring us to drama; they just narrow the field from which to create drama. So if the class suggests 'Let's do a play about Florence Nightingale', the teacher's thinking has to take a shift of gear to a perspective on Florence Nightingale that implies a tension which may further imply a potential learning area. So a different kind of categorisation might be:

Scutari hospital:
How do you write a letter for an illiterate soldier?
How do you cope with the smell of putrid flesh?
Who is in charge?
How do you cope when you have been on your feet for twelve hours and no-one takes over for night duty?
If you are a doctor and an officer, how do you cope with untrained women around?
This is an intrusion of women into a man's world.
This is a place where you help people to die.
Women who have never left England before journey to a totally different part of the world out of a sense of duty or as a means of escape.

All these are loaded categories; loaded in emotional directions: towards implications for dramatic tension, attitudes and sometimes actions. They are clumsy conceptual categories in that they vary in degrees of specificity, and in their potential for immediate role play, but what they have in common is the implied requirement that the participants in the drama will need to find some feeling value. There is nothing regulative about such a shift in gear; another teacher's list of aspects of Florence Nightingale might draw on quite different imagery or indicate a higher or lower degree of abstraction. Let us contrast the thinking of two hypothetical teachers on 'Ships':

Teacher A
1 Putting your faith in a vessel so small in a sea so big.

2 A journey is a looking forward; there is no going back.
3 Only *one* man is Captain, whether the ship sails or sinks.

Teacher B

1 Your hands may be numb and the skin raw, but you pull on that rope and you don't let go.
2 What do you write in your diary when you can't see the coastline any more?
3 You can see by the way the colour of the ocean bed is changing that the Captain is heading for a reef, but you keep your mouth shut.

Teachers A and B have both found a level of thinking loaded with emotional implications, so although interestingly different, both have a drama potential. The difference is in degree of specificity. Some teachers tend to think first as 'B' and then as 'A' or vice versa; some tend to confine themselves to one or the other; some cannot start drama at all because their thinking is limited to objective classifications. Indeed most of our training in educational institutions, particularly in further and higher education, is towards objectivity. It is not surprising that university students turning to teaching find it very difficult to think with their hearts. Such teachers may find themselves relying on their classes to know what is dramatic.

But even when your thinking tends towards that of Teacher A or B, or a mixture of the two, you have still further to go to reach drama. For the very notion of *categorising* experience in this way even with its overtones of tension and implied values is still a barrier to entry to the art form. This is not an easy topic to discuss and it may be that I am confusing my reader rather than clarifying for I cannot assume that there is a 'model' somewhere of teacher-thinking which we only need to adopt and all will be plain sailing. I am really trying to explain something that is partially only explicable in its own art form terms, within and through the action of drama itself. However, let us press on, bearing in mind the tentativeness of the arguments.

Concretisation

In the last few paragraphs action has been discussed in terms

144

of its specificity. We will now look at it in terms of its universality. The common way to regard an action or an object is to see it as an instance of its class: posting a letter is an instance of 'posting letter' activities or as an example of a range of activities that people do: posting a letter, running for a bus, and so on. The alternative way, crucial to the dramatic art form, is to see the action or object not as an instance but as a representation. It symbolises something much bigger than itself, something held in common by mankind, something about which people share feelings.

The drama teacher must perceive action and object as resonators of meaning. The action of posting a letter must evoke more than its functional meaning; it must be a crystallisation of, say, an irrevocable intercommunicating act. It is not enough for a drama teacher to make subjective classifications: he must think in terms of an action or object that will be both particular and universal. The implied actions of teacher B's list on 'Ships' must have the power to generate the thoughts and feelings that are nearer to and beyond the abstractions of the A list. Faced with a drama about soldiers, a teacher can enumerate many instances of what a soldier normally does, from making his bed or cleaning his weapons out of action to twisting his bayonet or setting fuses in action, but can he help his class set up the selected action in such a way that they not only find a feeling quality that will give the action immediate credibility, but also sense a bigger meaning than the action itself?

Obviously, when some piece of drama is starting, actions may remain functional, but the important thing is that the teacher's thinking never loses touch with the potential power within the most pedestrian action. This is where teacher role play, for all its variety of uses to do with challenging, giving confidence, promoting belief, setting style and building tension, is at its most effective. For the teacher in role can establish through the use of gesture, tone of voice, physical stance, choice of language, both the particular and the universal. This is the most important kind of teacher 'thinking', to think on one's feet, in role, to particularise and universalise at the same time. So that as, for example, his fellow outlaws talk about buying back their freedom, teacher (in role) lifts high the piece of gold that is his share of the loot, and ponders on whether you can ever be free of your past. His fellow outlaws may or may not take the bait and share this level of thinking with him. The important thing is that by working inside the creative experience along with the children, the teacher can offer that and other bait, and they will take it when they are ready. If the teacher stays on the outside of the experience, he cannot make the offer. That does not imply that he is never on the outside – it is very important that at times he should even appear to abdicate – but if he is to make Type D drama effective he will very often work from inside the creative process.

But if the teacher is to become skilled in all these levels of thinking, what about the pupils? Very often it is vital for the teacher to share this mental flexibility with his classes, and to train them in the skills. They too must know when it is important to categorise, to reflect on feeling, to find a universality, to seek an analogy and to particularise in an action that crystallises many layers of meaning. And they must learn to share this switchback thinking with each other. It is in itself a valuable class experience. What they need is a teacher who will reflect back to them the levels of thought they are trying out.

One of the most useful forms of reflecting back their ideas, their hunches, their feelings and abstractions because it is a way of sharing and publicly testing their thinking, is to use the blackboard. Thus the drama teacher of today carries a piece of chalk in his hand!

Appendix I
Football violence –
perspective one

An example of misunderstanding of the difference between conflict and tension occurred recently when I was working with a class of adults who set up for themselves what they assumed would be a powerful improvisation on attitudes to football violence. The context was a meeting of representatives of various local bodies (town councillors, youth clubs, football club, local residents, the police). They anticipated a lively discussion would ensue from such obviously conflicting standpoints. So it did, but they were not into drama – just a simulated discussion. Indeed it is fairly typical for teachers to assume that the introduction of some topical 'problem' is all that is needed to get the drama off the ground.

All they have supplied however is *content*, for *conflict is content, not form*. The theatrical form of tension still has to be set up. If the context in the 'football violence' *has* to be a meeting then the tension must be something to do with being at a meeting, so that the meeting takes on a reality, so that the roles they are attempting to play become credible and only then can the 'topical problem' become absorbed into drama. There needs to be a shared second dimension, for example:

1 That they must be careful what they say as the meeting has roused national press interest.
2 That the television cameras are there so they are on public view.
3 A sense of helplessness and hopelessness in dealing with an impossible problem.
4 A terrible sense of responsibility – the meeting has been called because a young girl is lying in hospital with concussion as a result of last Saturday's violence. The latest press report is read out at the beginning of the meeting.

147

5 'This chairman dominated the procedures at the last meeting; we shall not let that happen this time.'
6 Some people are already late for another meeting.
Any one of these 'tensions' will allow, even within the conflict of disagreement, a shared emotional reference point. This supplies the form in which the drama can develop. Notice that they can range from the 'heavily significant' (3 and 4) to the trivial (6).

Appendix II
Football violence –
perspective two

A lesson at Highfield Comprehensive School, Felling, Gateshead

The previous week this class of first year mixed-ability comprehensive school pupils had chosen as the topic for their drama: Football Riots. It so happened that the football loyalties of this school community were split between Newcastle and Sunderland; in this particular class they were split somewhat unevenly – about fifteen to eight. I had asked them whether in 'the play' they wanted to keep to this division, pointing out that it might be hard on the minority group if they did. They did! I also wanted to know from them whether the 'rioting' kick was something:

(*a*) they needed to get out of their system; *or*

(*b*) postpone; *or*

(*c*) take it for granted that it had already taken place or that we would be people not actually involved.

Only two hands supported (*c*). The rest of the class divided evenly between (*a*) and (*b*).

My first step had been (after a discussion of what started riots) to set up an exercise (in pairs) where the context was to be two of each opposition accidentally meeting before or after a match and starting trouble. I had stressed that this was an exercise and not the 'play proper', an exercise tha￼ would allow us to examine some of the features of ri￼ situations. I warned them that they would only need tw￼ three minutes to find these out and that I would sto￼ action. They would then be required to analyse wh￼ ments had been present and report back to the wh￼

This beginning of action had served the follow￼

1 It allowed them to 'scuffle about', but in a cor￼ text (controlled by numbers – only in tw￼

by time – only two minutes; controlled by purpose – an intellectual goal of examining its features).

2 It allowed me to observe *how* they would cope with simulated aggression (or indeed if it was not simulated!)

3 It established that this teacher's drama (I was new to them) would be characterised by a sense of purposeful work, even when the topic was as apparently unlike work as 'a riot at a football match'.

4 It allowed me time to ponder over what could usefully be abstracted as a learning area.

It seemed to me that some of the possibilities were as follows:

1 Causes and consequences.

2 Its meaning: a weekly ritual; mindless destruction; a vehicle for hate, for kicks; bit of adventure; a confirmation of group identity.

3 What happens to the innocent?

4 The views and responsibilities of the authorities.

Watching these twelve-year-old children in their parts, with obvious respect for each other, 'playing at being aggressive', I felt they were the innocents, that they had chosen the topic either simply 'for fun' or because they were apprehensive of the real situation which they no doubt experienced vicariously through the actions of some of the older boys (their heroes?) in the school.

I was not at all sure that with these children I was capable of setting up the violence of 'a real' football riot or even that I wanted to. The learning area I selected, therefore, was 'that individuals can lose their individuality in a group – they can behave differently and can be perceived differently'.

Even as the class discussed the features that had been present in their 'riot' exercise (a provocation, non-verbal signals, verbal signals, not wanting to be the one to stop the incident once it has started etc.) it emerged that the missing features were the real degree of hostility and the group influence. I indicated that it was the latter that we would look at next lesson but that I could make no promises that 'our play' would really contain the violence they knew to be ntral to the experience.

This may have disappointed them – I don't know. I knew that the theme I had now chosen, the differences between group and individual behaviour could hopefully emerge as a focus, however near or not near to the hostile reality our play took us: if *as a group* in the football match context, they merely became 'rowdy' or 'excited' or 'silly' or 'mindless' the point about losing one's individuality could still be underlined.

I now had to plan the next lesson.

The planning progress

A. The 'riot' action
A whole class of twelve-year-olds 'rioting' was not something I looked forward to. Somehow it must be controlled. The kind of constraint one can often impose on a 'battle scene' – each side selecting its own Goliath, limiting the number of weapons, distance created between the two sides by the use of projectiles like arrows or shot or the emphasis on the techniques of a sword fight – seemed not available here. The controls that were available seemed to be:
1 Some built-in psychological control relevant to the play, e.g. not everyone willing to fight.
2 Teacher in the role, either as a participant (no way!) or as an 'intervener'.
3 The degree of control exercised in the steps taken up to the moment of 'fighting' having some carry-over into the 'fighting' itself.
4 Some 'external' control like 'avoiding touching each other'.
    The last control (4) I could not even consider, but I mention it here because I know that in some secondary schools pupils are trained from their first drama lessons to evolve a technique of fighting without touching. When they reach a stage of using that technique without having to think about it any more it is very effective. It means that the pitch of hostile feeling can be very high, so that there is a strong sense of reality, but no-one gets hurt. But it only works with classes who are trained. For me to impose this out of the

blue would have been intolerable. I must in these circumstances rely on the children finding their own 'fighting' conventions.

The first three controls I could use but they must also satisfy *both* B. Credibility and C. The learning area.

B. Credibility

I had a choice: to discuss with the class what a believable context might be or to impose one on them. I chose the latter. My reasons were as follows:

1 Because we were to look at the influence of group behaviour the significance of that behaviour must be highlighted by there being something special about the occasion.
2 The difficulties of creating belief that one is driven to riot *while watching a match* I see as enormous.
3 Belief in the event is dependent to a large extent on the way we build it up in our minds, so *anticipating* it is going to be important.
4 They needed to share the same kind of anticipatory experience of 'getting there', so having a local derby at either Roker Park or St James's Park would not give a sense of 'groupness' as they would logically arrive by separate ways.
5 'Going away' to a match – a day coach trip – to a Cup Final derby in fact: two buses, a Sunderland and a Newcastle chasing each other down the M1 to Wembley might well be the way to symbolise the competitiveness between the supporters and the anticipation of a great event.

I was to handle what is for me as a teacher a difficult topic: I dared not risk diminishing the learning potential by leaving it to the class to tell me what the specific context should be. So I now decided to impose on them a 'getting to Wembley by coach context' and, additionally, finding themselves at the end of two abnormally long queues which because of some delay in getting through the turn-stile had edged into a quiet terraced street. The two lots of supporters would find themselves eyeing each other from separate pavements.

I also knew I needed to utilise two other symbols of competitiveness – scarves (I sent a message to the class the day before to bring them) and 'chants' (I made the mistake in the actual lesson of calling them 'songs' a semantic error which gave a weak start to credibility).

C. The learning area
How people behave differently away from their peers.
How perception of a group is influenced by a group identity rather than the separate identities of its members.

An experience meeting the requirements of the first statement demands that the pupils experience two contexts – group and individual. I *must not*, in order to achieve the latter experience, send them off into groups to create scenes that would reveal an individual's common-sense or anti-aggression values, or whatever, for that kind of subtle revelation requires more delicate pinpointing than most adolescents are capable of (and yet one sees just this kind of structure in a great deal of drama teaching in our secondary schools.) I needed to find a way that guarantees and brings out the individual's position in a way that is authentic for the pupils and economical.

I chose to turn the class into an audience, both at the beginning and the end of the lesson. Using two pupils who volunteered to be children who had no intentions of making trouble at the match I would role-play their respective fathers – one a doubter who, the day before the match 'threatened' his offspring about getting into trouble and who could not recognise that his child, in fact, had no intention of so doing; and the other a father who, although anxious, respected his child's determination not to get himself involved.

I felt it was also important for all the children, not just the two volunteers, to be conscious of their intentions so that they could then examine what changes had been wrought by the 'riot'. To this end I would get each child to commit to paper the degree to which he intended to get into or resist trouble on this great day. (In fact this was a dubious step · it is only ultimately effective if a useful proportion comm themselves to making trouble – otherwise you will have riot [and no play] on your hands – and if a useful propo·

commit themselves to *not* making trouble so that they experience having good intentions broken.)

My use of teacher-intervention in role would be staged at a point when the riot in the quiet street had got going. I needed to find some role intervention that in other non-group circumstances would be unprovocative but would have the opposite effect on a roused group; that perhaps in normal circumstances would engender sympathy but in these circumstances would not even be listened to. Damage to someone's roses in the front garden? An inhabitant of the street who was ill? It must be something that signals itself straightaway without being so explicit they are bound to take notice. I planned to hold a bandage-like object over my eyes and, from an upstairs window, appeal for quiet.

The lesson

It was very cold in the drama studio. The class arrived looking cold. Although I had not intended to start this way I let them play one game literally to 'warm-up'.

There were a few absentees, a few extras from last week; some had brought their supporter scarves. They sat round my chair with some sense of anticipation. As far as 'the play for them' was concerned this was to be a 'football riot'. I straightaway split them (still sitting on the floor) into Sunderland and Newcastle groups – only six Sunderland supporters as it turned out. I explained what the context would be: going to Wembley. I asked for two volunteers to be non-trouble-makers. A girl and a boy offered. I role-played their fathers in turn, playing the more threatening father with the girl rather than stereotyping the tougher approach with the boy. When the girl under my threats 'gave-in' and offered not to go on the bus, I had to stop the role-play in order to explain again that she should resist whatever I said.

After they had committed their intentions secretly to paper which they folded and placed in a pile, I got each group to practise its football chants ready for our coach trip to

Wembley. I *narrated* the journey, conducting them into singing as a kind of punctuation of the narration, using the image of one or other of the buses drawing ahead as a symbol of the competition that would be present in the game. During the narration the children sat on the floor, a black-and-white scarf and a red-and-white scarf marking the bus areas between which had been placed their 'pile of intentions'.

These same scarves marked the street positions of the two queues. My narration came to an end with 'during the boring wait, they sang again to keep up their spirits . . .'

But here I had made an error in my planning. Having held such a tight rein for various useful (I think) reasons I should have anticipated that they needed to know that the narration mode was over and that 'dramatic playing' could begin, that the responsibility was now switching for the time being from teacher to pupils. Had I warned them that I would abdicate at some point they could have taken up the reins with ease (they were a capable class). Instead we got an embarrassed hiatus which with a less able class might have irrecoverably dissipated energy and credibility.

Gradually by using a provocative 'aggressive neighbour' stereotyped role and withdrawing physically into a corner of the studio, I established that they could take a free hand and they started to use the situation to barrack each other 'across the street' and eventually 'fight'. It was not very real, but real enough to feed on my second role of the 'neighbour' with a handkerchief over his eyes. Their response was to ignore what I was trying to say by shouting me down. It reached a peak of rowdiness when I interrupted strongly with a new narration.

The scarves now marked the two police station cells to which they, according to my narration, had been carried off as a result of a phone-call from the inhabitant with bad eyes. I then asked a volunteer to switch to being a policema interviewing me, the complainant, between the two ce Cutting a pathetic figure (!), I told my sob story of he had just been released from hospital after an eye ope and I couldn't stand noise. This interview was held continual interruptions and barracking from eith which increased as the policeman led me out of the station.

Once I had left, the 'inmates' went through a succession of jeering at the policeman, hurling abuse at each other across the space between the cells and finally pleading with the policeman to let them out before the match started – which after some deliberation he did. It was interesting to notice that although the class had reached quite a pitch of excitement at this point it was kept firmly within the rules of the drama game.

Only five minutes of the lesson left – two vitally important things to do. Once they were free of their cells I switched the scene to school on Monday morning where I played the irate headmaster who *blamed them all* for causing trouble and then switched to the two children's homes where, if the drama experience had any potential of learning at all for that class, the scene where the boy who had answered his father that he would keep out of trouble stared back at his father silently under questioning should have encapsulated that learning. That was the key moment of the lesson as far as I was concerned: the success of all my planning depended on what that scene meant to them. All I know is that they watched it with rapt attention.

It did not matter at that moment whether in the play they had chosen to have the same intentions as the boy (in fact as it turned out from questioning afterwards that the majority had opted for making trouble). What did matter was what the scene meant to them, whether they identified with the impossibility of that boy's situation.

This was not a great drama experience by any means. Parts were not achieving very much at all. What it did provide, however, is a number of very important reference points for teacher and class. For some children it may have done nothing more than reinforce, unconsciously, what they already knew; educational value nil. For others it may have clarified something for them; if this is so then I would claim the experience to have been worthwhile.

Glossary

These terms are defined as they are used in this publication.

Abstracting   a process of selecting a dimension of the objective world.

Action   the activity of drama. Two aspects:
Internal action: covert activity (thinking, feeling etc.)
External action: overt activity (movement, speech).

Actual concrete context   What is actually happening to the participants.

Agent   the child or the teacher who controls the instrumental 'I am making it happen' aspect of dramatic playing.

Analogy   a parallel to the main issue – a means of distancing.

Art form in drama   a dramatic structure having a potential for shared significant experience.

Collectivity   a shared reference both at cognitive and affective levels.

Compatibility   the degree to which the actual emotional network of the class matches the emotional tone of the fictitious context.

Concrete action   activity that uses time and space.

Congruence   the degree to which the feeling quality brought to the fictitious context by the participants matches their intellectual grasp of that context.

Drama   Four types of orientations of drama teaching in schools:

Type A: Exercise, a short term, structured form.
Type B: Dramatic playing, a 'living-through' experien more loosely structured than exercise.
Type C: Theatre, a performance orientation, a struc form.
Type D: a special combination of all three of th

Existential used here synonymously with 'living-through' emphasising the passive, 'it is happening to me here and now' function of dramatic playing.

Fictitious concrete context the fictitious point of reference in the external action.

Focus selection within a drama.

Instrumental function the regulatory aspect of dramatic play: 'I am making it happen.'

Mantle of the expert a form of drama which stresses the responsibility that goes with knowledge.

Metaphor a dialectic between two contexts, the actual and the fictitious.

Objective meaning skills; facts; knowledge amenable to categorisation.

Particularisation moving from the general or abstract to the concrete.

Pivot a term used by L.S. Vygotsky to suggest the means by which action becomes subordinated to meaning.

Play for the class; Play for the teacher a model that implies two distinct movements in terms of both intention and structure.

Plot the sequence of events in the external action.

Practice play play where there is no fictitious element.

Role play using one's own person to bring an absent context into the here and now, in order to create a metaphor.

Stages Four stages in potential for change of understanding:

1 Artificial – no learning.
2 Reinforcement – unconscious reiteration of values.
3 Clarification – values made explicit.
4 Modification – some kind of change in values.

Subjective meaning a feeling-appraisal of the objective world; a personal value given to the objective world.

Symbolic play play where there is a make-believe or fictitious element.

Symbolisation a process whereby objects and actions accrue more significant levels of meaning for the participants.

Symbolism using one thing to stand for another. Piaget distinguishes two kinds: primary, where the child is conscious of the meaning; secondary, where the child is not conscious of the meaning.

Tension in inequilibrium – related to both a psychological state and to dramatic form.

Theme the underlying meaning; meaning related to the internal action.

Title a label a participant might choose to apply to the drama.

Bibliography

ALLEN, JOHN (1979) *Drama in Schools: its theory and practice*, Heinemann

BERGER, PETER L. and LUCKMAN, THOMAS (1972) 'Language and knowledge in everyday life' in *Language in Education* Open University set book, Routledge and Kegan Paul

BOLTON, GAVIN M. (1977) 'Creative drama as an art form', *London Drama*, Apr. 1977

BOLTON, GAVIN M. (1978a) 'The process of symbolisation in improvised drama', *Young Drama*. Feb. 1978, **6**. 1

BOLTON, GAVIN M. (1978b) 'The concept of showing', *Young Drama*, Oct. 1978, **6**. 3

BRUNER, JEROME S. (1974) *The Relevance of Education*, Penguin

BRUNER, J.S., JOLLY, A. and SYLVA, K. (eds.) (1976) *Play: its development and evolution*, Penguin

DAY, CHRISTOPHER (1975) *Drama in the Upper and Middle School*, Batsford

FINES, JOHN and VERRIER, RAY (1974) *The Drama of History*, New University Press

GILLHAM, GEOFFREY (1974) 'Condercum School Report' for Newcastle upon Tyne LEA (unpublished)

LANGER, SUSANNE (1953) *Feeling and Form: a theory of art*, Routledge and Kegan Paul

LANGER, SUSANNE (1963) *Learning in a New Key*, Harvard University Press

MCGREGOR, LYN, ROBINSON, KEN AND TATE, MAGGIE (1977) *Learning Through Drama*, Heinemann

O'NEILL, C.C. *et al.* (1976) *Drama Guidelines*, Heinemann

O'TOOLE, JOHN (1976) *Theatre in Education*, Hodder and Stoughton

PIAGET, JEAN (1972) *Play, Dreams and Imitations*, Routledge and Kegan Paul

SLADE, PETER (1954) *Child Drama*, University of London Press

STABLER, TOM (1979) *Drama in Primary Schools*, Macmillan

VYGOTSKY, LEV S. (1933) 'Play and its role in the mental development of the child' in Bruner *et al*. 1976

WAGNER, BETTY J. (1974) 'Evoking gut-level drama' in *Learning, The Magazine for Creative Teaching*, March

WAGNER, BETTY J. (1976) *Dorothy Heathcote: Drama as a Learning Medium*. A National Educational Association Publication

WARNOCK, MARY (1976) *Imagination*, Faber

WATKINS, BRIAN (1974) 'The game of drama', Birmingham Polytechnic (unpublished)

WAY, BRIAN (1967) *Development Through Drama*, Longman

WHORF, B.L. (1966) *Language Thought and Reality* ed. J.B. Carroll, MIT, Cambridge, Mass.

WILKINSON, ANDREW (1971) *The Foundations of Language*, Oxford University Press

WITKIN, ROBERT W. (1974) *Intelligence of Feeling*, Heinemann

WHITTAM, PENNY (1977) *Teaching Speech and Drama in the Infant School*, Ward Lock